LIES *at the* ALTAR

LIES

at the

ALTAR

THE TRUTH ABOUT GREAT MARRIAGES

Dr. Robin L. Smith

New York

Copyright © 2006 Dr. Robin L. Smith

Library of Congress Cataloging-in-Publication Data

Smith, Robin L.
    Lies at the altar : the truth about great marriages / Robin L. Smith.—1st ed.
      p. cm.
    Includes index.
    ISBN 1-4013-0256-4
    1. Marriage. 2. Married people—Psychology. 3. Marriage counselling. I. Title.
HQ734.S743 2006
646.7'8—dc22   2005046795

Design by Renato Stanisic

FIRST EDITION

10 9 8 7

This book is dedicated to

Ms. Oprah Winfrey
FOR SO FREELY GIFTING ME WITH THE
OPPORTUNITY TO LIVE IN THE LIGHT,
WARMTH, SAFETY, AND JOY OF THE TRUTH—
AND FOR BEING THE BRIDGE THAT BROUGHT
ME BACK TO MY TRUEST SELF.

To FEARLESS WON!
THE LIFTER OF MY HEAD, MY REFUGE
AND MY STRENGTH, MY JOY, MY GUIDING STAR IN
DARKNESS, AND THE LOVER OF MY LIFE AND MY SOUL!

CONTENTS

CONTENTS

ACKNOWLEDGMENTS

As a writer, I find this section humbling, because with each word I am more in touch with what a village it took to birth this book, and the arresting competence and profound love and support that surrounded this labor of liberation and love.

I first want to thank Catherine Whitney, whose brilliance helped me capture each essential nuance for this book, whose spirit was steady, easy, and overflowing with generosity and kindness. I bow to your literary competence, and am filled each time we speak with the flowering of a professional relationship that I hope will last a lifetime, and a new trusting friendship, which I treasure. I look forward to entering the kitchen of creativity with you and cooking up my next book with you by my side. Thank you for everything! I also am deeply grateful for the special contribution to the writing and spirit of this book made by your collaborative partner, Paul Krafin. He provided a valuable perspective and sensitivity.

While the book is dedicated to Ms. Oprah Winfrey, this is where I get to say more. Oprah, thank you for being at ground zero, not only for the birth of *Lies at the Altar*, but for my new birth. You entered the sacred rubble of both this book and my life, and reminded me to make the decision to live my best life. I hope you know that without you, this book would not be the gentle alarm clock, the new liberation song for couples, and the invitation to new life for people everywhere. I am so grateful that the divine order is always on time. Thank you for fully supporting me, for respecting my gifts, and for introducing me to the world!

As I thank Oprah, I want to express my gratitude as well to the whole Harpo family, which has welcomed me with such warmth and excitement. In particular, I am thankful to several individuals who gave invaluable help to this book: To executive producer Ellen Rakieten and your staff, for nurturing this project and keeping your hand in the mix when your own schedules were so demanding elsewhere. You were always available and generous with your input, and made sure the end product was flawless. To Harriet Seitler, who made the first move with "the call" that I will always remember as the beginning of a ride better and bigger than anything my heart had dreamed possible.

I am thankful to the phenomenal team that made the cover of this book a true reflection of who I am and the invitation I am making to others: Lisa Halliday, who coordinated the photo shoot and made sure that all was well; Andre Walker for creating "the hair" for the cover of this book, and for your seasoned expertise, your hands of magic, and your gentle, quiet, and wonderfully reassuring spirit; Reggie Wells, for taking my face and creating a portrait of welcoming ease, approachability, and beauty. Your eyes saw an image of me that I couldn't see myself, your fierce clarity let me know from the gate I was in the hands of a master, and your humor kept my heart laughing; and Kelly Hurliman, the clothing stylist, who was so calm and reassuring. Kelly invited me to feel comfortable, safe, and exhilarated in my body.

To John Madere, photographer extraordinaire. With each shot your skilled eye found the best in me and called forth my aliveness. You invited a freedom of expression, and told me without speaking many words to let my liberation and joy be made known to all. You captured a free, relaxed, joyful, and secure me. I hope to work with you again!

To Gayle King, editor-at-large at *O* magazine, for cheering me on. Thank you for being happy for me. It means a lot. And to the supportive people at the magazine, especially editor-in-chief Amy Gross, and writer Aimee Lee Ball.

To my Hyperion family, I am grateful for each person who offered their oh-so-seasoned skills and expertise to create *Lies at the Altar*. First, to Robert Miller. Bob, thank you for wrestling with me in the light. I treasure the way you always shared your thoughts, feelings, and beliefs, while respecting and welcoming mine. From our first meeting in the halls of Harpo Studios, you understood my concept and pursued with excitement and vigor the publishing of *Lies at the Altar*. You believe that the message of living in truth is an essential foundation for creating great marriages and great human beings, and your commitment to that goal has been an inspiration to me.

To my editor, Leslie Wells, whose reputation as "the best" is well-deserved. Although you came on board after we had started this journey, you immediately claimed our vision as your own. Your savvy, soothing, encouraging, and expert stewardship has been a blessing. Thanks, too, to Ellen Archer, William Schwalbe, Phil Rose, and Miriam Wenger. Special thanks to Mary Ellen O'Neill, the editor who gave this project the spark of life before moving on to do other great things in the world of publishing.

To Jane Dystel, my literary agent. I have said this to you privately, but a public proclamation is in order. We were meant to be. I honor your counsel, your seasoned experience and expertise, and appreciate your value, trust, and respect for my creative artistry and my intuitive knowing.

To Miriam Goderich, for your attention to detail and willingness to explore my wish and desire list. And to all the other people at Dystel and Goderich Literary Management, whose support of this project from start to finish has been a source of comfort and strength.

To Mary Beth H. Gray, Esq., my chief legal counsel. Mary Beth, I love your brilliant legal mind, your scrupulous attention to detail, and your gentle, strong spirit. You are not only my attorney but my trusted friend. Thanks for walking with me through many seasons of my life.

To David S. Rasner, Esq., for making sure that all was well, and for firmly supporting me.

I am humbled that Dr. Harville Hendrix, one of the great giants in the field of healing marriages and helping people understand how childhood hurts impact their lives, cheating them of their birthright to joy and wholeness, was willing to endorse *Lies at the Altar*. Dr. Hendrix, your kindness, support, and belief in my work, as well as your willingness to lend your name to this project was the desired cherry on top. It added an unexpected sweetness to this sacred subject. You are a true pioneer, and paved the way for this book to build on the concepts of your Imago Relationship Therapy and further share its healing and transforming potential with the world. Thank you for lighting the way for me!

A special thank you to Sunny Shulkin, LCSW, for being a wisdom guru and a powerhouse of honed knowledge and insight. You have always generously shared your brilliance and your profound understanding of the human condition and intimate partnerships with me. Also, thank you for introducing me to Imago Therapy many years ago, and for ultimately being my connection to Dr. Hendrix.

A very special thank you to the women who participated in my focus group. Your courage, insight, openness, raw honesty, and willingness to be vulnerable helped tremendously to shape this book. I consider your contributions to be among the most sacred revelations I have ever witnessed in a public forum. I commend each of you for sharing your stories, your pain, your struggles, and your triumphs with me and with the group. I will always be grateful for your priceless gift of honesty, openness, and resilience.

To the young people at the Youth Study Center in Philadelphia, a juvenile correction facility. Thanks for cheering me on, and for reminding me why it is so important that adults get it right—that we parent you better, love you deeper, help you to heal the hurts that we have caused you, and enable you to become mature and healthy role models of what love, commitment, and marriage can be. You remind me of how important it is to learn to repair ourselves when we are broken. I honor your journeys, respect your pain, and carry you in my heart always!

To Dr. Howard C. Stevenson, Jr. You are my friend, my brother, my colleague, a freedom fighter, a bold professor, prolific researcher, highly skilled clinician, and a person I hold in the highest regard. Our work together has shaped me and found a meaningful voice in this book. I have been deeply influenced by your living example of integrated brilliance with application. I love sitting at your feet and learning; it is one of my prized treasures.

To my clients and patients, and all those whom I have learned from. Your stories of pain and progress, of trials and triumphs, of tears, fears, and recovery, have loaned me courage as you allowed me to witness your bravery and vulnerabilities. And to the strangers who encourage me to keep sharing the message, to write more books, to share the light of what I have learned—I have heard you and I have responded. Thank you!

To my parents: My father, Warren E. Smith, M.D., who died in 1990; and my mother, Rosa Lee Smith, MSS, who has blessed me with your zest for life and your love of learning. Your devotion and support of me and your gentle love for Kalle has enabled me to pursue the work I've been put on the planet to do. I honor your forty-two years of marriage, the example of excellence lived before me, and your willingness to struggle with me as I grew into the life that is uniquely mine to live. I so honor my father, who knew I had it in me to go the distance and who fully embraced my aspirations. He always believed in me and nurtured my dreams. I can still hear the echo of his voice gently reassuring me that if I did my part, my dreams would one day come true. He planted the seeds of compassion, peace, hard work, discipline, integrity, and success, and taught me by example how to live a life of meaning. My love for each of you runs deep and wide. To my siblings, Damian and Joy, who have each supported me in their own unique ways, and to my extended family who is always in the wings cheering me on.

To Kim, my assistant, thank you for keeping my schedule straight, and for reminding me to "find that place." Your help, expertise, and laughter are invaluable to me.

To my core inner circle of dear friends; you know who you are. The candle holders of my life, who lifted lanterns of love as I walked the dimly lit road back to myself. Who rocked and sang to me, reminding me of who I was when my memory failed me, and surrounding me with a shield of safety as I recovered my divine birthright. You danced with me until the rain of joy, fullness, and abundance bathed me, and until the terror in my eyes had washed away. To this very special group of people who play with me, pray with me, and stay with me—you have my heart, and my profound gratitude.

To Pia Mellody, RN, CSAC, and Terrence Real, MSW, two of the best therapists around. You understand the world of pain, trauma, depression, addiction, and recovery. The seeds you planted in my life continue to flower with bright brilliant colors and the sweet fragrance of peace, boldness, and well-being.

To my pain, my private tutor, which I finally listened to, and to the midnight hours of ache from which this work was birthed, I am grateful to you. Joy and peace are now part of how and who I learn from. They are my close companions.

To Kalle, my joy, the love of my life, my daughter, and an exquisite Portuguese water dog. You make every day of life special, full of sweetness and the best laughter ever. You are pure love and God's truest gift to me. Mommy so loves you!

And, pulling up the rear, always having my back, the foundation of my life and the circumference of my being—God! I thank You for simply giving me a life of abundance above anything I could ask for or imagine. You are a lamp for my feet and a light for my path. Most of all I thank You for witnessing my life, and for allowing me to truly know that I am non-erasable and irreplaceable to You. That knowledge and understanding has transformed me. Thank You for loving me with an everlasting love . . . and I love You back!

LIES *at the* ALTAR

True to Myself

Let me begin with the truth. I have known what it is to live a lie—to want so badly to keep a relationship that I made myself invisible. I have known the exhaustion of trying to hold up a facade that has no foundation. So in this book, I will not be speaking from an elevated position. I will not be telling you what I *think* but what I *know*.

Truth is what holds my life together now. It is not an accessory. It is a necessity. As with a credit card, I never leave home without it. But I walked through the darkness of lies to get there. I would like to spare the pain of every woman who fears that she can have love only if she erases her needs and makes herself small. I would like to shout it from the rooftops and mountain peaks that truth is better, warmer, stronger. It is the only way to have a great marriage or a great relationship.

I was once in a long relationship with a man whose addiction ruled our lives. The breakup was devastating and deeply painful. But even more painful than leaving was facing the truth of why I had stayed for so long. Why I had remained with a man whose love and loyalty were devoted to his addictions. Why I had lied to myself while enabling his lies to flourish. As his lies blossomed, I was being killed softly. Life—real living—had stopped for me. The self I thought I had was evaporating. I was slowly but surely fading away. I no longer recognized myself—and how could I? I was no longer there.

Each day I laid out his disguise for him, made certain his false front was neatly in place, his cover-up richly textured, logical, and foolproof. I allowed him to lie to me about who he really was and what he really valued, and I stood by while he lied to everyone who thought they knew him so well.

Being with this man almost killed me—almost crushed my bright and resilient spirit and tampered with my sturdy and robust mind. He wanted to rob me of my very essence, and for a long time I let him. Where was I in my life that I could have devoted so much time, energy, and effort to a man who neither honored nor valued me? How had I, a highly trained professional with what I thought were nearly flawless intuitive skills, become involved with such an impostor?

Why did I stay in a relationship with a man who could hurt me so deeply, who could make me feel ashamed of wanting a normal life? How could I think it was okay to be with someone who taunted me and prodded at the open wounds of my insecurities? He told me I wasn't much of a woman, and he criticized me relentlessly. I gave away my power, thinking it would soothe him, and it did temporarily. But each day required that less and less of me exist. I tried to be better, tried to be happier. I made meals out of crumbs and smiled as I ate the crumbs in order to appear full and satisfied. I tried to be more understanding and accepting. I was looking for a way to make something work that made no sense. I realize now that, with all of my effort and devotion, he never really saw me, much less loved me. When he grew tired of the way my desire for connection collided with his desire for oblivion, he simply erased me—from his cell phone, from our post office box, from his life— and replaced me with another woman and a new life.

Being erased was my worst nightmare—literally. It also saved my life. That moment of utter, unassailable truth sent me reeling, but I was grasping for the light. For the first time in my life, I asked myself: *Am I enough for myself? Can I be unerasable?*

I was raised in a family in which women (very *smart* women, I might add) existed only in the reflection of strong and successful men. While, fortunately, most of these men happened to be kind (like my father), it was nonetheless painful to be a nonperson. We all learned to be very good at mastering the frozen smile and learning how to warm a room with smiles that had been plastered there by history. The important thing was to keep the relationship, because it was the only way we believed we could be significant enough to exist. Pretending was our modus operandi. We could drink cyanide and call it Kool-Aid, that's how good we were at self-deceit. And that's how I later came to walk around in the dark and call it light. I was taught to do just that. I wasn't sure what was real and what wasn't real. I didn't know if I could stand in the winter of aloneness and create my own warmth.

I am grateful to say that the old family themes and patterns holding us hostage can be broken. And once that happens, it is possible to create a firm foundation of truth on which to build a life and a marriage.

Once I decided to stop letting lies dominate me, I had to get down to the business of walking in truth, no matter how difficult the road or how long the journey. I knew that if I aligned myself with the truth, I would be guided, supported, and connected, and I was right. Walking in truth has radically changed the landscape of my life. I have made a covenant with myself. I have vowed to stand at the altar of truth and commit myself to plain and simple honesty. I have chosen to make my most important life partner the truth.

Today I would only want to be with a man who respects and honors me, and whom I can respect and honor. I would want to be with a man wise enough not to lose everything for an addiction. I would never be with someone who needed to choose between me and a substance or another woman. I would only be with a man who is sexually and emotionally faithful because it's part of his value system, a man who chooses to live more in truth than in lies because truth lives in the very fiber of his being.

This book is my invitation to you to make the same choice. But you must begin with an inner healing to achieve a wholeness that the world did not give to you—and that once you have, no one can take away. It belongs to you, like a company in which you hold one hundred percent of the stock.

Join me in this journey of discovery, allowing curiosity to befriend you, and leaving shame and criticism behind. If you make this investment in yourself, you will receive the largest return of your life: You will get the real *you* back. You'll never again be put up for sale, or traded like a commodity. As sole owner of your life, you will make the wise decisions as to where and how you share and spend your emotional, spiritual, financial, physical, and sexual wealth. You are worth this investment. And worthy of living your best life.

One

"WHEN I DISCOVER
WHO I AM, I'LL BE FREE."
—*Ralph Ellison*

From This Day Forward

It was a beautiful day for a wedding. The church was packed with happy family and friends. The bride was stunning in an ivory satin wedding dress, the groom elegant in a fitted black tuxedo. The wedding party circled them in a color-coordinated cloud of taffeta and tails. As the couple stood before the silver-haired minister, they gazed deeply into each other's eyes. Then they each spoke the vows they had written themselves:

"You will be my best friend," she pledged, "except for Marcia, who will always be my *very, very* best friend. And my German shepherd, Spike, who will sleep at the foot of our bed."

"I promise to take care of you and want only what's good for you," he replied, "as long as it works for me and doesn't involve frequent visits from your mother."

"I'll treasure you for who you are," she said, "but once we're married, I'll expect you to drink less, work harder, start showing an interest in the arts, and shave off that beard."

"What is mine will be yours," he responded, "except for the money you don't know about and the cash I'll sock away in a private account, just in case things don't work out."

"I promise to love you unconditionally," she said, "until you do something I find intolerable; to forgive and forget, although you know I come from a family of championship grudge-holders;

and to never go to sleep angry, although I may have to stay awake all night fuming."

"I'll adore you forever, in body and soul," he said, "as long as you keep that gorgeous size-six figure."

"I promise to cherish you every day for as long as we both shall live," she answered, her eyes welling with joyous tears. "Or as long as I can stand to put up with you."

This exchange may sound comical, but often as I am counseling troubled couples, I find that similar thoughts and "but-ifs" were lingering just beneath the surface of their wedding vows. They made promises they could not keep and said flowery words they did not fully understand or believe, hoping that the magical aura of their lavish wedding would carry them through their lives and make everything okay.

What was going on? They were lying at the altar, lying down on the job of forging true partnerships, making up stories that they hoped would someday come true. They were swept out on the sea of love, carried away on a tide of sentimentality and emotion that would sooner or later return them to life's rocky shore in a crushing wave of reality. They were bystanders at their own wedding, speaking vows they wrote themselves without ever acknowledging the truth about their relationship and their real lives. They traded one glorious day for years of bitter struggle. At least half of these marriages would not survive to the tenth anniversary. Many others would stick together, serving their time until death, locked in a prison of their own design, never comprehending how unions that began with such optimism and joy could go so horribly wrong.

How can it be that people who want only to be happy can end up so completely miserable? What are the lies at the altar?

NAMING THE LIE

A dear friend of mine recently ended a marriage after fourteen years and three children. The man Cheryl chose as her husband was wrong for her in every way. Harold had problems with addictions, he was unfaithful, he was manipulative and cruel. Now divorced, Cheryl was tormented that she could have made such a terrible choice. "What on earth was I thinking?" she asked me. "How could I have married this man?"

"You were just standing there lying at the altar," I said. "Not because you were bad, but because you didn't know what you were saying."

She was shocked. "Lying" is a harsh word, and Cheryl insisted that she had really believed her wedding vows: "I meant it when I promised to be with him until death." She added quietly, "And it almost killed me."

What was Cheryl's lie? It wasn't conscious or deliberate. It was the result of unconsciousness. Her lie began with the self-deception that Harold was not really who he appeared to be. Cheryl is one of the sweetest, most caring women I've ever known. She always looks for the good in other people, which is a wonderful quality. But when you trust someone who has proved himself untrustworthy, you're choosing a dangerous form of blindness. Harold telegraphed his true nature loud and clear before they were married, and Cheryl didn't see it. He was mean and controlling, and he showed little concern for Cheryl's feelings. Even after they were engaged, he'd disappear for days at a time without telling her where he was, and Cheryl had reason to suspect he was with other women. When she tried to ask him about it, he'd accuse her of suffocating him. Once he said, "We're not even married yet, and already you're putting a noose around my neck." Cheryl always backed down, feeling silly for saying anything, and this is when the self-doubt began to build a home in her mind, spirit, and heart. This is when she made the lie into the truth. The pattern would repeat itself throughout their marriage. Harold did whatever he wanted to do, and Cheryl learned not to challenge him because he always made her feel like a fool when she did.

Cheryl had been raised to believe that a woman had to work hard to be desirable to a man. Her father had made her feel unworthy, with frequent taunts that nobody would want to marry her if she stepped out of line. Harold continued the pattern, blaming

Cheryl when he became withdrawn or angry. "You drive me away," he'd tell her to explain his absences. "You make me so mad, no wonder I need to drink."

Cheryl took his words to heart and kept trying to do more and more to please him. Harold could not be pleased. "He constantly made critical little comments about how I kept house or took care of the children," Cheryl said. "I just never felt as if I was good enough."

Cheryl cried when she recalled a particularly overwhelming period shortly after she'd given birth to their third child. "It was Sunday, and I always cooked a big dinner that day. After we ate, Harold went and plopped on the couch in front of the TV. It was getting late, I was exhausted, and there was so much to do. I had a new baby, a toddler, and a four-year-old running around. So I asked Harold if he could help me by bathing the older children. He didn't even look up from the show he was watching. He just said, 'I don't feel like it.'"

Cheryl remembered that day in particular because she so rarely asked Harold for help, and she'd asked only out of desperation and exhaustion. His indifference cut her deeply. "I went straight into the bathroom and I cried like a baby," she recalled. "Then I wiped my face and went downstairs and cleaned up the kitchen. After I finished, I gave the kids their baths and put them to bed."

Cheryl felt real despair that day, but it took her fourteen years of the same treatment to finally leave Harold. Why so long? Because she had made a sacred vow at the altar, and she refused to break that vow. She didn't understand that a promise made to someone who isn't even there, who cannot reciprocate, is an empty promise.

Harold's lie was more direct. He promised to love, honor, and cherish Cheryl, but only as long as she put his needs first and allowed him to do anything he wanted. And here's the real lie: Even when she complied, he gave her nothing in return. He never expressed appreciation. He never told her she was beautiful. He never hugged her or said he loved her.

It took enormous courage for Cheryl to admit the truth and file for divorce. Harold never did get it. "Do you think someone else is actually going to want you?" he said derisively as she walked out the door. She didn't bother to answer. What was the point?

TRUTH: THE SECRET INGREDIENT

Let's agree that it's time for the truth. From this day forward.

Even if you've been hiding your real feelings for many years, burying your needs, harboring resentments, and deliberately denying what you know, you can make the choice to change. It doesn't matter if you've had a string of failed relationships, if you're suffering in a marriage that isn't working, or if you're divorced and hope to try again someday.

You can finally make a conscious effort to lay that heavy burden down. And here's an amazing fact: Hard as it is to believe, you can find love in the course of facing the truth. It's the secret ingredient to every great marriage.

Maybe you are planning your wedding as you read this, and have hopes of love everlasting. You want to know how to avoid the constant power struggles and unhappiness you've seen in the marriages of your friends and family. If you ever hope to live happily, you'll have to trust in the truth. You'll have to believe that facing the truth is going to get you a lot closer to living a life full of joy than the lies. In fact, truth is the *only* way to create lasting love, security, and real passion.

Let me help you. The truth *will* set you free.

WAKE UP TO YOURSELF

A lot of the time it just feels easier to curl up with a fantasy than to wake up to reality. But once you do wake up, it's hard to go back to sleep. And the longer you stay in a state of wakefulness, the better and more natural it feels.

The first step is to begin looking at your relationship—the one you have now or one that failed in the past—and ask yourself some basic questions. This examination may expose painful realities, but try to avoid feelings of shame or blame. Shame ("I'm a bad person") provides a comfort zone for many people. It becomes an excuse to give up. Blame ("He or she is a bad person") may feel temporarily satisfying, but it doesn't get you closer to the truth. Shame and blame are relationship exits. They kill your dreams, your spirit, and your passion. I invite you to stay in the room and stay awake.

As you read the following Top Ten Lies and corresponding truths, learn to recognize the difference between the lie and the truth, and do a reality check in your own life.

1. LIE: *If the package is beautifully wrapped, its contents will be fabulous.*

TRUTH: *The packaging doesn't tell you anything about what's inside.*

"She's not really my type," my friend Gerald said of Irma, the woman he had been dating for five years. I was surprised to hear it. Gerald and Irma had always seemed very much in sync. They were both committed to community activism, enjoyed working on the old house they'd bought together, loved children, and had similar senses of humor. Irma got along well with Gerald's large family, and he was close to her parents.

"You and Irma seem great together," I said. "Tell me what you mean when you say she's not your type."

Gerald shrugged. "I don't know. I always thought I'd be with someone different. I prefer petite women, because I'm not so tall, and Irma is a couple inches taller than me. Also, I always saw myself with more of an artistic type, not an accountant like Irma."

"Are you serious?" I asked, thinking he was kidding. He wasn't. When he broke up with Irma a few months later, she was stunned. So were their families and all of their friends. While Irma nursed her broken heart, Gerald began dating a dancer he met at a party. She was petite, artistic, and ten years younger than Irma. Within six months Gerald and the dancer were married.

It was no great shock when Gerald called me a year later, wanting to talk about his marriage. "It's like living in a war zone," he said bitterly. "She fights with me about everything. She hates the house, she refuses to spend time with my family, and all she ever wants to do is hang out with her stupid dancer friends. Now she tells me she doesn't want children."

I was sorry to see Gerald in so much pain, but it was the inevitable outcome of his fantasy. He'd chosen his ideal package, but when he opened it up, he didn't like the real woman inside. Sadly, she wasn't his type at all.

Most people don't intend to be shallow about choosing a mate. The facade is important, because it's what you see in the first moment of attraction. It's also terribly seductive. When a beautiful woman or a dashing man chooses you, that's heady. When your partner is wealthy, accomplished, or famous, you feel elevated. These feelings are not wrong. The problem is, many people don't dig any deeper than that.

A woman I know broke up with a man she'd been seeing for several years. They had been engaged to be married, but it just hadn't worked out. Their parting was amicable, and I asked if they would remain friends. She said, "No. He's not someone I ever would have chosen as a friend." I thought, *Wow!* She'd been engaged to marry someone who wasn't even her friend. Their attraction was only skin-deep.

If you fall in love with his dreamy blue eyes or her silken auburn hair, there's a rude awakening ahead. If you are not marrying the soul of your partner, there will be nothing to hold you together when the facade becomes less appealing. Trust me. It will. I think of the woman who sat in my office, crying her eyes out because her husband of six years had told her he was physically repulsed by her. She'd been slender when they married, but had gained about twenty pounds during two pregnancies. He took it as a personal affront, saying, "You knew when we got married that being overweight was a deal breaker."

Life brings hardships, sickness, aging, and stresses that are beyond our ability to predict. Bodies sag and hair thins. People want to put their best face forward when they're courting, but you need to be able to see each other as you are beneath the facade.

Ask yourself: Do you like what you see on the *inside* as much as what you see on the *outside*?

---

2. LIE: *The past is over.*

TRUTH: *The past is driving you to the chapel.*

"My real life starts on my wedding day," Stacey told me firmly, explaining why she wasn't going to tell her fiancé, Frank, about the child she'd borne out of wedlock and given up for adoption when she was sixteen. She wanted to permanently shut the door on her old mistakes and start life fresh with the man she loved.

"The question is, *why* are you not telling him?" I asked. "Do you worry that he'll think less of you? Will he consider it shameful, when in actuality it is sacred and meaningful? What does that say about him? About you? Why would you be willing to go underground with your own sacred story?"

Stacey had hoped that she could present herself at the altar, "new and improved," without the baggage of her past. Life doesn't work that way. When we say, "My life starts here," we deny the reality that the past is the limousine driving us to the chapel.

After our conversation, Stacey decided to tell Frank about the baby. It was a big risk, because although she trusted him, she felt her secret was so big it could cancel everything out. Later, she called me to tell me what had happened. Her voice was shaking.

"He hugged me," she exclaimed, and she started crying. "He said, 'That must have been so hard for you.'" She couldn't believe Frank's response—his capacity for empathy. In an instant, it changed her life and lifted her shame. Stacey had been unaware that her shame was not something *he* evoked, but what she had carried with her as a result of her own family's response to her teenage pregnancy and adoption. I call it shame being paid forward.

A couple came to see me on the verge of separation. Amy said she didn't trust her husband, John. When I tried to get to the bottom of what had triggered her lack of trust, it was revealed that John had told a big lie at the beginning of their relationship. Although he had been married and divorced twice, he'd told Amy he'd been married only once. He was afraid she wouldn't be interested in him if she knew the truth. Unfortunately, Amy found out about his second marriage at the worst possible time—when they applied for a marriage license. She was shocked but didn't put on the brakes. She didn't say, "Wait a minute. Who are you, really? Let's delay the wedding for a few months while I find out."

She convinced herself that his lie didn't matter. The wedding proceeded as planned. But from the first day of their marriage, she couldn't trust John. He, in turn, hid other details from her.

"I don't mean to lie," he said, "but . . . I don't know." John looked at me helplessly.

"You're afraid if she knows the real you, she won't want you," I said.

He shrugged, not knowing how to answer. Amy broke in. "Don't you see it's the lies that bother me?" she asked John. She was ready for the truth, recognizing it was the key to intimacy. In the coming months, Amy would show John that he was safe with her and didn't have to fear abandonment.

It's a fantasy that the past doesn't have to be reckoned with, doesn't have to be folded into the relationship. I'm not saying you owe your partner a complete recount of everything you've ever done. But if you're hiding the important milestones, you're leaving out essential pieces of yourself. And if you don't deal with your past, your past will deal with *you*. As Dr. Harville Hendrix, one of the most respected gurus of relationship therapy and the creator of Imago Relationship Therapy, so powerfully illuminates, most of the destructive power struggles that couples engage in are the result of unresolved childhood wounds and disappointments.

Ask yourself: Do you present yourself fully and honestly,
or do you live in dread that your partner
will find out about the "real" you?

3. LIE: *Anything is better than being alone.*

TRUTH: *Being alone and free is better than
being together and controlled.*

Charlene had been divorced for ten years and was raising her daughter alone. All of the responsibility rested heavily on her shoulders. She was always worrying about making ends meet and was constantly scrambling for babysitters when she had to work late. At night, exhausted, she would lie in her bed and quietly cry because she was so tired of carrying the burden alone. Then she met a man who seemed strong and confident. He swept into her life and told her that he would take care of everything. She was so relieved. She completely gave herself up to him. Finally, she could let go. But she didn't recognize that someone being controlling is not the same as someone being loving and supportive. She soon began to resent his control. She bristled at his high expectations. Her new marriage suddenly felt suffocating.

As Charlene tried to understand how she'd gotten herself into this mess, it slowly became clear to her. It was as if she'd been on a long road trip, driving her car down an endless highway late at night. She had become so tired that she'd pulled over to the side of the road to rest, feeling that she couldn't go on. And then someone had almost magically appeared and said, "Close your eyes. Rest. Don't worry. I'll drive." And she was able to let go and fall into a deep, luxurious sleep. It felt so good! When she woke up, fully rested, she was ready to drive again. She wanted to take the wheel, wanted to share the fun and even the burden of driving, but things had changed. The new driver said, "No. I'll drive. You just sleep some more." And when she argued that she didn't need any more sleep, her new partner just patted her hand, smiled knowingly, and kept driving. "Falling asleep at the wheel" took on a whole new meaning for Charlene.

Ask yourself: Are you awake and fully participating
in your relationship, or have you abdicated
control due to exhaustion or fear?

---

4. LIE: *You have to go along to get along.*

TRUTH: *In a great marriage, you can ask for what
you need without fear of rejection.*

I come from a nice family. That is to say, putting a nice face on things is given a high value. As children, we were encouraged to put others first. That meant playing with kids we didn't like because they were lonely, or excusing unkind behavior because the perpetrator was having problems at home. As a result, I never learned to fully value my own needs, and I was too easily persuaded that I didn't really want or need what I thought I wanted or needed. I learned to do mental gymnastics that would have qualified me for the Olympics if "playing pretend" were a category: pretending to be happy when I wasn't, pretending to be grateful for crumbs when I'd earned a full meal. Almost reflexively, I'd give the other person *more* than the benefit of the doubt, thinking, *Well, maybe he has a point,* even when my insides were churning, my deepest intuition screaming out, "No, no!" At last, a close analyst friend told me bluntly, "Robin, you're allowed to have preferences." As that point sank in, it was like being set free. I didn't have to play with someone I didn't like? Do things I didn't want to do? I no longer had to convince myself that I enjoyed the party life when a quiet night at home was more my style. I remember a friend of mine sharing that although she loved going to jazz clubs, she feared her boyfriend would consider her a snob if she admitted she loved the symphony, too. In the movie *Runaway Bride,* Julia Roberts plays a woman who doesn't know how she likes her eggs because she's always ordered them the way the man in her life preferred them. What sets us up for such inner confusion and selflessness?

The challenge is to find out what your true preferences are, examine them, and then own them so you can offer the real you.

Ask yourself: Does your partner love and respect your differences or demean the things you like and make your preferences feel silly or snobbish or crazy?

---

5. LIE: *It's important to be right.*

TRUTH: *It's more important to relate authentically.*

When you marry, you are forming a brand-new union that has never existed before. You're entering unmapped territory, which can be both exciting and scary. In the unknown, it's human nature to reach for something familiar as a guide. As you draw the new map of your union, you'll be referring often to your familiar family maps. That's okay, even valuable. This is your first opportunity to learn something about yourself and your partner. But what happens if one partner announces that his or her personal family map is going to be used as the authority for the marriage? Instead of redrawing the map to fit the parameters of the territory, he wants to force the territory to shape itself around a predrawn map. The inflexible partner is saying, in effect, "That's the way my family always did it, and it worked for us." This stalemate in itself reflects the partner's blind spot. This type of ignorance and arrogance will cheat a couple of their ability to have a mature marriage built on the shared values of truth, respect, and love.

The inability to integrate new information into the marriage map is part of what kills marriages. I call it the arrogance of being right. I often ask couples who are stuck in intractable positions, "Do you want to be right, or do you want a relationship?" They almost always say, "We want a relationship." After all, that's why they're sitting in my office. But the truth often is that they want to be right. How do I know? After weeks and months of talk, neither has budged from their initial position. Our sessions are devoted to their finding new ways of explaining and justifying their separate points of view. Change is not an option. They're merely waiting for the other person to cry, "Okay. I give up. Uncle!"

In his revolutionary research on what makes marriages last,

Dr. John Gottman has found that one of the key predictors of a successful marriage is the ability to be open to your partner's influence. This doesn't mean being wishy-washy or easily controlled. It means being open to new information, being willing to redraw the marital map to accommodate the other person's input, and being willing to accept the gift of expanding your worldview because of your partner's influence.

Ask yourself: Are you or your partner more interested in being right than in being in a relationship?

---

6. LIE: *You can learn to live with compromises that trouble your soul and make you suffer, and call it love.*

TRUTH: *Suffering is not love.*

When Martha met Theo, she was fifty-three years old, and she felt strong and clear about her needs. She'd been divorced for seven years from a man she'd married quite young. "I made all the usual mistakes," she said. "I got married right out of college, and neither of us knew who we were or what we wanted. By the time we realized we didn't want each other, we had two kids. The divorce was extremely hard, but it was the right decision for both of us.

"When I met Theo, I knew my needs. I had my list of negotiable and nonnegotiable items, but I just somehow got unplugged from them. I kept telling myself things were acceptable when they weren't."

In a three-year period, Martha watched her nonnegotiable list shrink to nothing. There were always extenuating circumstances, and she stretched her mind to the snapping point trying to accommodate Theo.

When he refused to let her daughter and new granddaughter visit for a week because he couldn't stand the noise and mess of having a baby around, she told her daughter not to come, even though she had so looked forward to being a grandmother and missed spending time with her daughter.

When he got into an argument with their best friends and cut them off, she cried and pleaded with him to make up, but when he refused, she reluctantly went along with him.

When he constantly drank too much, she blamed the stress at work, even though she'd vowed never to marry a man with a drinking problem.

"My world was shrinking into a hard little ball," Martha said, "but I kept telling myself he was worth it."

"Worth the obliteration of your happiness?" I asked. "Worth the alienation of your friends and children? Worth losing your self-respect?"

Martha was ashamed that she had so easily forsaken her needs once she married Theo, but she didn't want to be alone again. She comforted herself with the justification that marriage was about compromise and she could live with her compromises. Then one day Theo suggested that because their marriage was good in every way but sexually, he could have sex outside the marriage and take the pressure off her. "I actually found myself contemplating it," she said. "That's when I realized I had completely lost my inner compass."

I often find that people, especially women, enter marriage without knowing what their needs are or how to ask for what they want. But even when you know your needs, it's easy to get sidetracked if you are driven by fear of rejection, loneliness, or conflict.

Ask yourself: Have you made concessions that once would have seemed unthinkable, or accepted the unacceptable out of fear?

---

7. LIE: *"It's you and me against the world."*

TRUTH: *You can't have a great marriage if you live in a bunker.*

I was in a department store one day when I ran into an old friend of my mother's whom I hadn't seen in years. Mary looked wonderful. She stood straighter, somehow, and her eyes were shining. She was wearing a fashionable red suit.

Mary greeted me with a big smile and a hug, then told me, to my shock, that her husband, George, had died three months earlier. "Oh, Mary," I said, "I'm so sorry. I hadn't heard."

"It's all right, Robin," she said. "I'm not grieving. In fact, I'm back in school getting my master's degree in women's history. I plan to teach. I'm doing fine. In fact, I'm doing more than fine."

She hesitated before saying boldly, "I'm liberated. For fifty-five years, I was George's servant, his slave. I gave him my whole life. And now whatever years I have left are going to be about me. I feel no grief. I am relieved. I'm glad I have a little time left on the planet to focus on myself."

I appreciated Mary's brutal honesty, but her words made me sad. To think that such a vibrant woman had surrendered decades of her precious life this way, and I'd never noticed it. She'd been good at keeping her secret. She'd been locked in her bunker with a cruel taskmaster, and even her closest friends hadn't known.

If your partner demands that you cut your ties, if your world becomes smaller because you are in love, if shame and fear drive you inside, you cannot have a great marriage. The isolation keeps you well defended. In secret, in the darkness, you don't have to show your pain. Once you speak of it and bring it into the light, you are required to face it.

Ask yourself: Is your love expansive and free, or does it cut you off from the oxygen of the world?

---

8. LIE: *If you believe in the same God, you'll share the same values.*

TRUTH: *Values are what you* live, *not what you* believe.

What does it really mean to share values? People have said to me that they married someone who was in their church, synagogue, or mosque because they had the same values, but then discovered the other person wasn't kind or considerate of others. I've heard from people who married a person who had the same political ideology only to be surprised when the politically correct spouse was less tolerant in private.

Values go deeper than religious affiliation or political party. They're the DNA—the Dominant Natural Attitude—of your relationship. They are reflected in the way you approach life, whether you are optimistic or bitter, giving or selfish, open-minded or narrow, judgmental or forgiving.

Julie was raised in a large, religious family. Her mother had impressed upon her daughters that she had been with only one man in her life—their father—and that this was a sign of high moral character. Julie wanted to be able to tell her future children that she'd been with only one man in her life, so when she had sex with Robert, she knew she had to marry him, thereby guaranteeing that she maintain the moral righteousness that would make her a role model for her children.

In the coming years, she was able to tell her daughters, as her mother had told her, that the only man she'd been with was their father. She could not, however, tell them why Daddy was so mean, or why he stayed out late so many nights, or why she cried so much.

Ask yourself: Do your partner's attitudes and behavior in the world exhilarate and inspire you, or do they make your stomach churn and drain your spirit?

---

9. LIE: *Marriage magically changes people for the better.*

TRUTH: *The person at the altar will be the person at the breakfast table.*

How many of us go to the altar believing that the sanctification of marriage will change our partner for the better? Some might call it faith. I call it resolute denial.

If he is controlling before the wedding, what makes you think he won't be controlling after the wedding?

If she doesn't enjoy sex before the wedding, what makes you think she'll enjoy sex after the wedding?

If he has trouble keeping a job before the wedding, what makes you think he can keep a job after the wedding?

If she drinks too much before the wedding, what makes you think she'll drink less after the wedding?

If your partner were missing a leg, you wouldn't say, "I hope she grows a leg." You would say, "I'm marrying somebody who has only one leg." But we don't always apply this logic to our intimate lives. When it comes to marriage, we can act as if people who are emotionally lifeless, spiritually empty, mean, or selfish are going to transform themselves after the wedding and grow relationship legs. We don't see them for who they actually are. It is vital that we do!

Ask yourself: Do you love the person you see today, or the person you hope he or she will become after you've pressured, nagged, begged, and tormented him or her into changing?

---

10. LIE: *Marriage is an automatic ticket to self-esteem.*

TRUTH: *You have to be whole before you can be joined.*

"I thought he was nice enough," Gillian said of the man she married. "Nice enough!" She shook her head in disbelief that she could have accepted that. "I wasn't in love when I got married to Sam. I felt no passion for him. I think I got married because I was twenty-nine and didn't know if I'd get another chance. The men I had loved the most had dumped me. So I thought this was perhaps the best I could do."

Now forty-three and the mother of a thirteen-year-old daughter, Gillian was depressed at how the years had slipped by without improvement in the relationship. I asked her why she went to the altar with a man she didn't love.

"I think this goes back to my low self-esteem, particularly around body image," she admitted. "I was fat as a kid, and although I had slimmed down quite a bit, I still had a lot of cellulite, and

I thought I was flabby. When a relationship would end, I always felt it was because men wanted someone with a better body, even though nobody ever said so."

On some level, Gillian believed that marriage would make her safe and lift her self-esteem. She and Sam were the picture of a solid couple in public, but in private there was no real connection. Theirs was a cool, formal relationship; even the sex was perfunctory. Gillian knew that Sam had had at least two affairs during their marriage, and she'd often thought about leaving him but had stayed for the sake of their daughter, and because she believed that no one else would want her.

"Tell me something," I said gently. "Would you want your daughter to have a marriage like yours?"

Gillian seemed startled by the question, then she burst into tears. The question had touched a nerve. When Gillian envisioned her daughter living such an arid life, she was horrified.

"Why do you think *you* deserve it?" I asked.

It was a breakthrough moment for Gillian.

If you can answer yes to this question, and you *would* want your child to have a marriage like yours, that's wonderful. But if your answer is no, you have to think about what that means and how you're going to make a change, so your son or daughter does not witness marriage as a place of sadness, submission, or the abdication of personal identity.

Ask yourself: Does your marriage lift
you up or hold you down?

SUFFERING THE CONSEQUENCES

Answering these questions without blame or shame is a good first step in taking an honest look at yourself and your relationship. You may discover hidden lies that prevent you from achieving the happiness and intimacy you seek. What are you going to do with that knowledge?

You have three choices:

- Continue to suffer.
- Look outside your marriage or relationship to get your fantasy fix, which always leads to more pain, drama, and trauma.
- Choose to find out what can happen when you live in truth.

People often tell me that changing old ways seems too hard, or that they're too old to change. But nothing is more draining than trying to force a relationship into "happily ever after" when the truth is an unwelcome guest in your home. Know that the lies lead to pain, and the truth can open your life to happiness. If you are desperate to keep the illusion alive, you will suffer.

I often hear people say, "Marriage is a struggle," as if that's its primary purpose. I think of Rhonda and Edward, a middle-aged couple who came to me for counseling. They radiated unhappiness from every pore. She was angry. He was sullen. At the beginning of the session, Rhonda said that in spite of their problems, they were determined to fix their marriage. "I know that marriage is hard work," she said in a tone that communicated exactly how much heavy lifting she was required to do.

"What is the hard work?" I asked.

She looked puzzled. "What do you mean?"

"You said marriage was hard work," I replied. "What is the hard work?"

"You know," she said impatiently. "It's a struggle. Trying to get through the days, trying to get along."

"That is not the definition of marriage," I said. "That's the definition of suffering."

If you think of marriage as hard work, you need to ask yourself:

What is the goal of this hard work?

What is the payoff?

Marriage is not about "doing time." It is not a life sentence to pain, humiliation, and suffering. Nor is it a grueling job. Here's a piece of surprising news: Love really doesn't hurt. A good marriage doesn't hurt.

Suffering occurs when the lies you bring to the relationship encounter the truth of what it means to live with another human being. If you believe that you enter a dream world on your wedding day, that you'll be lifted up and carried away on a white cloud, it will hurt like hell to be dropped back to earth. The only way to avoid the shock of pain and the residual ache that lingers for years is to give up the romantic fantasy and find your happiness in reality. Trust me, that's not as dreary as it sounds. Reality can be more exhilarating and passionate than any fairy tale.

There's nothing wrong with a romantic high. The surge of feeling is good. But you have to know that it can't last—and decide that a lifetime of joy must be built on a sturdier foundation.

In a real union, you can get your needs met. You can bear witness to each other and your life together, not as you pretend to be, but as you really are. Within the generous space of honest love, you have permission to exist and to allow your partner to exist. Fusion, or a blurred oneness, is not the requirement or the goal.

I was at a conference recently, and one of the speakers said, "Truth precedes love." *Bull's-eye!* I thought. Truth must precede love. Otherwise, what we think is love is just an illusion. The promise of truth is freedom. You can stand at the altar and say, "I'm not here because I feel forced to be here. I'm not here because I'll die without you. I'm not here because it's my last chance. I'm not here because my parents will be pleased, because everything is paid for, because I'm too embarrassed to back out. I'm here because I choose you. We stand exposed before each other. You *see* me. I *see* you. And we say, 'Yes!' It's an informed, full-fledged yes. We choose to be together." That's mature love.

This book is about helping you make better choices. If you're looking for a partner, if you're planning to marry, or if you're already married, and you feel like you're in a pit of unresolved misery, you can make your relationship more mutually satisfying and fulfilling. You can have a better tomorrow than you have today. You just have to show up for duty—the duty you have to yourself and your partner to build a marriage worth being in, worth your life, worth your breath.

"When I was a child, I spoke as
a child, I understood as
a child, I thought as a child.
But when I became an adult,
I put away childish things."
—*1 Corinthians 13:11*

Show Up and Grow Up

I got married when I was twenty-three to a man I'd dated since I was eighteen. I thought I was ready. I'd been on a fast track with my education and career. I graduated high school at sixteen, college at twenty, and had just completed my master's. My career plans were marching forward like a well-rehearsed band. I'd traveled around the world and had been exposed to life in all of its diversity. I thought I was mature. I graduated on a Saturday and got married the following Saturday.

My former husband is a really good man. Like me, he came from a stable and loving family. Both sets of parents had been married for over forty years. We stood at the altar with all of the confidence and expectation of young love.

We meant well, but we didn't have a clue about who we were, where we were headed, or what we were about to create. As I look at the pictures from that day, I see a young girl wearing a beautiful gown and a brilliant smile as she walked down the aisle on her father's arm. I see the desire in her eyes to have a happily-ever-after life as she posed beside her handsome husband. But I don't recognize her anymore. That girl may have been worldly in her own way, but she didn't understand what it meant to be married. She didn't know how to get her needs met or how to meet her husband's needs.

He loved me, but he was no more prepared than I was. Our marriage lasted only five years, and our divorce was traumatic, as all divorces are, but especially painful because we were such good friends, were so connected to each other's families, and had countless moments of pure joy. It was heartbreaking for each of us, a dissolution that caused a steady, constant ache. I think I can speak for both of us in saying it was a long journey into some form of maturity and healing. We were decent people, but we weren't grown-ups. Our vows were sincere, but they were ultimately promises that were not rooted in who we really were and what we really wanted and needed.

The first marriage vow should be: *I promise to show up as a grown-up.* Not as a little girl fulfilling a fantasy. Not as a nervous boy doing what he's supposed to do. Not as Prince Charming or Lady Bountiful. Not as the fulfillment of your mother's expectations. Not as the envy of all your friends.

Focus your eyes. Take a good look. Who is that person standing in front of you now? I'm not talking about the one you've dressed up to fulfill your idealized wedding dreams, or the one you expect to change to meet your desires once you're married, but the living man or woman of this moment.

Is the picture foggy? Are you treating your marriage as if it were a blind date? Going into it blindly? (Keep in mind that blind dates usually don't work out!) Do you have questions you're waiting to bring up after all the excitement dies down? Do you have significant doubts that you expect to be erased by the end of the ceremony? I have news for you. The time to see clearly and speak directly is now, before the wedding. I know what a tough thing that is for you to do. No one wants to throw a wrench into the works. I can empathize with how hard it is to get real and break the spell, to quench all of those warm, fuzzy feelings—not just your own but everyone else's, too. But telling the truth is the only way to claim the moment as mature adults and say: *My life matters . . . our lives together matter, and I respect you and me.*

Now, I want you to be aware that the modern wedding culture has set a trap for you. You have to be watchful. On your guard. It's not easy to be a grown-up when the world is pushing a child's fable. But the consequences of traveling that false road can be severe.

In the spring of 2005, the entire nation was riveted by the story of a Georgia woman named Jennifer Wilbanks, who became known as "the Runaway Bride." Jennifer disappeared a week before her wedding, triggering a massive nationwide search. It was assumed that the pretty bride-to-be had been abducted while she was out jogging. Everyone braced for a tragic ending. But then the standard script took a wild turn. Four days after Jennifer disappeared, she reemerged in Albuquerque, New Mexico. The public was stunned when the truth came out: Jennifer had indeed put on her running shoes that day, but she'd also tucked a bus ticket in her pocket. While her family and friends searched in vain, Jennifer was on a cross-country bus trip with no certain destination in mind. Simply put, she fled. Even her closest friends couldn't understand it. "She was so happy," they insisted. "They were the perfect couple. She was so excited about her wedding."

Jennifer had no words to explain her actions. Perhaps she'd been overwhelmed by the intensity of the wedding preparations, which involved eight bridal showers and twelve bridesmaids. Perhaps she'd been spooked by the sheer size of the event, with six hundred wedding guests expected to attend. Perhaps she was having second thoughts about getting married.

Many people wondered why Jennifer didn't just say it was all too much. Why did she have to put her family, her fiancé, her friends, even the nation through such a traumatic and expensive ordeal?

Maybe she tried to speak up and her concerns were deflected. Maybe she sent out a quiet cry for help and everyone was so preoc-cupied with the wedding preparations that nobody heard her. Maybe she was too ashamed to air her doubts because her friends were con-stantly telling her how lucky she was, how happy she should be. She was with a fabulous man from a prominent local family. It was re-ported that he adored her and would do anything for her. Did doing anything for her include hearing her doubts, seeing her angst, even if that meant calling off or postponing the wedding? Often the state-ment "I'll do anything for you because I love you" stops way short of hearing things that we don't want to hear. So in the end, maybe the pressure, the buildup of expectations, the investment made by her family and friends and his family and friends, the overwhelming cascade of events, the inevitability of it all, left Jennifer mute. If she spoke the truth, it would become reality. She couldn't speak, so she ran. And when she returned to Georgia, everyone found her flight so incomprehensible, so *crazy*, that her fiancé convinced her to check herself into a psychiatric hospital. There seemed to be no plausible explanation for her actions other than a complete nervous breakdown.

The truth? Jennifer probably *was* having a breakdown. Not *because* she ran but *before* she ran. Staying in a lie will do that to a person. While I'm not suggesting that using taxpayers' money and scaring her family and friends half to death is okay, I imagine Jennifer was trying to run more toward the truth than toward lies.

The modern wedding has morphed from a sacred ceremony into a theatrical spectacle. The focus is less on vows and the relationship than on rings, dresses, locations, invitations, flowers, food, cakes, bands, limos, videos, photos, showers, and honeymoons. The result: a day of fantasy, followed by a week or two of fantasy, followed by a lifetime of bang-you-in-the-face reality. Immersed in the preparations, the hapless bride- and groom-to-be are forced to say, in effect, "Darling, love of my life, I really don't have the time to hear you now and tell you how I feel, or have you tell me how you feel, but don't worry. We'll have time to fight each other tooth and nail for the next twenty-five years."

If there were a flashing sign, it would read: DANGER, DANGER. It's a setup for failure.

We need to pay attention to the values we're reinforcing when we portray the ideal wedding. We collude in the lie by supporting its continual airing. There is a program on The Learning Channel called *For Better or for Worse*. I tuned in one day to find the episode "The 100K Dream Wedding." A couple was given $100,000; their task was to spend every cent in one week's time to create an extravagant wedding. Could it be done? You bet. They spent an enormous sum on the location and the wedding dinner alone. Many thousands of dollars were spent on the flowers, which included the petals of ten thousand roses scattered along the aisle and down the front steps of the church. The bride gushed about her dream wedding. Dismayed, I wondered what this couple had learned, thanks to The Learning Channel. My guess would be they discovered that money buys a moment of what feels like happiness. Or at least that money buys garish excess and a chance to make sure everyone knows it. After all, it was filmed and edited, then shown on TV. Forget about intimacy. Their special day became a television event. I would have felt some relief for them if a portion of the money had gone into premarital counseling, but all of the money was spent on extravagance. There is nothing wrong with a beautiful ceremony that is built on the foundation of truth. But sometimes, the bigger the event, the more there is to hide. The opulence becomes a decoy to keep the attention on the glitter so the lies and hidden aches aren't noticed. In fairness to most brides, this is what women are socialized to do. The idea is reinforced again and again that the more over-the-top the wedding, the deeper the love. Although I am not a statistician, I do understand that nothing could be further from the truth. It's called an inverted relationship— as one side goes up, the other side goes down. As the required fanfare goes up, the focus on the quality of the internal relationship goes down. And keep in mind that whatever we focus on is what grows. So, if you focus on a magnificent wedding versus cultivating and planting the seeds for a magnificent and long-lasting marriage, you might get the wedding day of your dreams and the marriage of your nightmares.

I suppose it was inevitable that a reality show called *Bridezillas* would hit the tube. Shown on the Women's Entertainment network (WE), *Bridezillas* follows "high-maintenance" brides-to-be through their wedding preparations. The tag line for the show is "Watch real brides go from sweet to certifiable."

The brides in this program behave like spoiled children, and they believe their behavior is justified because this is, after all, "MY BIG DAY." They show up—do they ever!—but they are not grown-up. In one episode, we see a disappointed bride storming down the aisle, in a rage because the beleaguered wedding planner overlooked some minor detail. I have no doubt that as the bride spoke her vows, she wasn't thinking about her groom or the future they would share together. Instead, she was probably plotting her revenge against the wedding planner.

As a society, we have come to accept that weddings are events, the bigger the better. We think it's okay to go into serious debt, to spend two years organizing the location, the caterer, the flowers, the food, the band, the cake. And how much time is spent considering the vows or the underlying foundation on which the marriage is to stand?

When I told a friend about my idea for this book, she frowned and said, "Robin, you're trying to take away the dream." She was wrong. I believe in dreams. But the dream I want couples to share is the dream of a solid, real relationship, a relationship that will endure when the excitement dies down and it's just the two of them, alone together at last. We have to wake up to the fact that fantasy gets in the way of living. We have to acknowledge that the 50 percent divorce rate is a reality, because coming back down to earth hurts far too much. And by the way, of the 50 percent who remain married, too many are living far outside the vows of love, honor, and cherish. They're hurting, too.

Is your wedding already getting in the way of a happy marriage? It's an important question. But let's back up a minute. You have to be a grown-up before you even start courting.

TRUTH IN MATING

Beautiful dreamer seeks tall, handsome stranger
who is romantic, passionate, successful, worldly,
strong, and a good kisser.

Does this read like a typical personals ad? Yes, it does—if the ad were written by Sleeping Beauty. Many of us approach the altar with stars in our eyes, clinging to the dreams we've nurtured since childhood. We may be smart, stable, strong individuals when it comes to other areas of our lives, but the search for love and the quest for a ring make us all jiggly at the knees. The meaning of love and marriage gets mixed up with fairy-tale notions.

If you are looking for a Prince Charming to awaken you from the doldrums of your life with the power of his magical kiss, let me remind you that the fairy tale ends there. We aren't treated to a view of what life is like after the awakened beauty and her prince ride away on his stallion. What keeps fairy tales preserved in perfection is our ignorance of the rest of the story. For all we know, Sleeping Beauty later confronted Prince Charming with "Thanks for the kiss, but this really isn't working out for me." Or the prince may have said to her eventually, "I loved you when you were asleep, but I can't stand you now that you're awake."

Prince Charming doesn't exist, even if you're a real princess— as Diana discovered even before she married England's Prince Charles in the Wedding of the Century. Later, after the royal marriage had collapsed, Diana revealed that she'd considered canceling the wedding, but her friends persuaded her to go ahead, saying, "Your face is already on the tea towels."

I have talked to numerous women and men who swallowed their doubts before their wedding because the momentum of the event was too great. They chose to promise love and loyalty for the rest of their lives because they didn't want to disappoint their mothers, or they'd already sent out the invitations, or the hall was booked, or this was the first man their father really liked, or they were simply too embarrassed and too afraid to speak the truth. A lie at the altar seemed preferable. But more often than not, they were addicted to the romance of the whole thing.

It's true. This addiction is absolutely real, the result of a chemical cocktail stirred up by our hormones when we first fall in love. Those waves of passion and ecstasy coursing through our bodies are the product of a pronounced spike in dopamine, a hormone that produces feelings of pleasure, and norepinephrine, which is similar to adrenaline and increases excitement. Together, these chemicals create that exquisite lovesickness we experience in the early stages of love. Initial attraction is like a drug that detaches you from reality. You feel high, great, as if you could walk on air. The problem is that the drug is fast-acting, and it leaves your system quickly.

Some people find the thrill so intoxicating that they keep coming back for more. They're like drug addicts looking for another fix. They need the cocktail to feel normal. When things eventually settle down, and when the chemical reaction is diminished—which must happen in order for true love to mature and life to progress—withdrawal sets in. They wake up in the morning and no longer feel the charge of passion and giddiness, and they think that something is wrong with their relationship.

The romantic fantasy tells us that these feelings are a reliable measure of love, but this is not reality. You can't live fully in each moment if you're lovesick. You can't function well if you have a fever. In the intoxication of new love, our promises and passionate vows feel so noble and true. It's not that we don't believe them, only that they exist inside a most fragile bubble, and when that bubble bursts, we are left with nothing to hold on to. When the marriage falls flat, we blame each other or ourselves.

This stubborn refusal to give up the fantasy, even in the face of irrefutable evidence, reminds me of a friend finding out as a child that there was no Santa Claus. She knew the truth but didn't want to accept it. The fantasy was too wonderful. So she told her mother, "I know there's no Santa, but I want to believe it, so I'll still put out cookies and milk by the fireplace." It's a charming sentiment when voiced by a child, but a twisted idea for adults.

I've often counseled newly married couples who are mortified because they no longer feel any of the heat they think they're supposed to feel. People around them are saying, "Here come the lovebirds" or "They're still on their honeymoon," and they're not even speaking, let alone having sex anymore. They've lost the urge to merge and feel cheated and let down. They don't know how to love each other when they don't feel that ecstatic chemical surge.

Think about some of our most cherished images of love and imagine what life would be like if they never abated:

"I daydream about my love throughout the day."

"When I see my love, my heart leaps."

"When I'm not with him/her, I'm miserable."

"I long to make love with him/her all night, every night."

"I'm head over heels in love."

"I worship the ground he/she walks on."

"When he/she looks deep into my eyes, I melt."

"I love him/her more than life itself."

"I would do anything for him/her."

"She/he's my whole world."

Here's a radical idea: Maybe we don't want to be lovesick, because sickness—even such an exquisite one—makes us feel weak and uncomfortable and unable to cope. Ultimately, it makes us unstable. Maybe the vertigo that accompanies falling in love is meant to be short-lived, because otherwise we couldn't *live*. We were taught to want to be swept off our feet. To want to fall in love. But is *falling* really such a great sensation? Do we want to be flailing, unable to catch our breath, unsteady on our feet? I've grown to dislike the phrases "falling in love," "knocks me off my feet," and "swept away." The act of falling is hurtful and potentially hazardous. Being knocked off your feet or swept away is dangerous, and it leaves you hurt and vulnerable.

A woman I know lost her job because she took too much "lovesick leave." Jerry was a successful advertising executive in her mid-forties. She'd put off marriage because she'd never found that perfect match. As the years passed, she kept hoping. "I know he's out there," she told me once, gazing up at the sky as if she expected her true love to arrive from the heavens in the blaze of a meteor.

When Jerry met Eddie, she knew immediately that he was "The One." He was the most romantic man she'd ever met. He had eyes only for her, and Jerry felt thrilled to have found such a magnificent love. "It was worth waiting for," she assured me.

Jerry and Eddie were married, and Jerry was in a perpetual state of bliss. She found it hard to concentrate on her work, and in the first months of her marriage, it seemed that she was constantly apologizing to clients for missing deadlines or failing to return their calls. "I'm sorry," she'd tell them, "I just got married and I'm so happy, I've been a little distracted."

At first her clients and coworkers cut Jerry some slack. They liked her and were glad that she'd found love. But her work continued to suffer a precipitous decline in both output and quality.

One day her boss snapped at her, "Your happiness is getting in the way of my happiness." Jerry was fired.

Jerry was furious. "I worked my tail off for fifteen years," she complained to me, "and now, when I want some happiness for myself, they turn on me. What's even worse is that Eddie is upset that I lost my job. He thinks it was my fault. I feel like my boss just ruined my whole life."

My heart went out to Jerry for the hurt she was experiencing. The truth was so painful that she couldn't honestly look at it. She blamed her boss, and her husband blamed her.

"Let's take blame off the table," I said. "Blame is a cop-out. It doesn't help you out of your pain. Let's see what's really going on."

Later, Jerry would feel ashamed that she had allowed herself to get so carried away that she jeopardized her career. "What's wrong with me?" she cried.

"Don't let shame fill the hole in your heart," I urged her. "You're not a bad person. You're not weak. You were sleepwalking, and now you're awake. Let's focus on how you and Eddie can have a great marriage that is built on truth, a deeper understanding of the situation, and some compassion for all involved. And let's figure out what steps you can take to repair the damage to your career."

That was seven years ago. Today Jerry and Eddie are doing well because they chose to explore what mature love meant for them. They're not giddy or lovesick, and they have a much deeper level of intimacy than they had when they were crazy in love, tearing off each other's clothes every chance they got. The intimacy they have created and the passion that was birthed out of their crisis are far deeper and more satisfying than fleeting hormonal urges. Their connection is a fountain of living water that nourishes their relationship instead of draining it dry.

How much do feelings really have to do with a good solid marriage? Ask yourself what meaning you ascribe to feelings. Knowing that they change, what meaning will you give them when they do? Maybe you'll think the love is gone when it's just the initial intoxication that is diminished. Maybe you'll think you're with the wrong person and will betray your partner by having an affair to get the feeling back, only to discover that you're chasing a feeling that can't last. The initial infatuation that we call love isn't love at all. It is being *in love* with the idea of what we think love should be. People leave marriages, have affairs, and withdraw emotionally and physically because they confuse the illusion of love with true love.

Here's the truth: You are not powerless in the face of your feelings. You can choose what meaning you give to them. This is the lesson that most of us didn't learn in childhood, and that's why feelings scare us so much.

THE RING OF TRUTH

Helen was a fifty-year-old widow, contemplating marriage to a sixty-five-year-old man. She had never been to a therapist, but she took a chance because she needed to do a reality check. "I don't know if this is important or if I'm just being silly," she told me. "I haven't had much practice being engaged."

Helen had been widowed at forty-five, after being married since the age of seventeen. She didn't expect to ever get married again, but to her surprise, she'd met a man two years earlier, and their relationship had progressed to the point where he wanted to give her a ring. That was when the trouble started.

"Jack told me he was looking for just the right ring," she said. "I wanted to be a part of the process, and he basically told me he knew what he wanted. What *he* wanted. He took me to a jewelry store and told the saleslady, 'Show her what I think looks good.' I was shocked, embarrassed, and furious. It was just plain control. That's the way I saw it. I wanted to show him what I liked, and he called me a spoiled princess. Anyone who knows me knows that's preposterous."

As she told the story, Helen became increasingly indignant. Then she thrust out her left hand to show me a large diamond ring that overpowered her small hand. "He went ahead and got the ring he knew I hated, and the other night he presented it to me."

"And you accepted it?" I asked.

"Yes, but I'm wondering if I can stand to wear it. Or stand to be with a man who is so controlling." She took a deep breath. "Maybe I'm making too much of this. It's just a ring. I love him, and it might be my only chance."

"Are there other ways that he is controlling?" I asked, knowing the answer would be yes. A man so intent on dismissing Helen's preferences about her engagement ring was sure to show up with regular control issues.

Helen acknowledged that Jack was a man who "knows his mind." But most of the time, it didn't bother her too much. The ring bothered her. It had made her sit up and pay attention, because it symbolized not love, but control.

"Tell me," I said, "where else in your life have you been criticized for asking for what you wanted, and have ended up cooperating because you didn't want to make a fuss?"

"That's easy," she said. "My father was that way. I always did what he wanted me to do. When I was in high school, I got pregnant. I was told I had to get married, so I graduated on Monday and got married on Friday. I stood there six months pregnant in a blue smock in my living room. And I remember the vows. I took them very seriously, as I heard them. I felt like a little child, you know, being reprimanded and spoken to harshly by the principal. And I tried to live those vows. I tried to the point of almost killing myself, because my husband was also very demanding. So now, when I know I'm supposed to be excited, I'm not feeling that way. I guess I think I'm entitled to have what I want at this point in my life. I've always put everyone else's needs first, and now it's turned into a battle to get my needs met. I feel the same pressure I felt as a child to give in to get along and be kept around."

"You're being pressured to show joy for something that doesn't represent you," I said. "You're supposed to be happy about a ring that you had nothing to do with, that goes against your wishes, that doesn't reflect your taste. And if you express unhappiness, you're told you're acting spoiled, which you know is a lie." I smiled sympathetically. "What a bind that is for you, having to be happy about something that doesn't make you happy. And you're wondering how you can celebrate something that doesn't exist."

Helen left my office, still unsure about what she would do. She called me the following week and said she had confronted Jack about hating the ring. "He said, 'Can't you just lie to me and say you like it?'" She sounded sad. "I don't want to marry a man who thinks it's okay if I just pretend to be happy—who *wants* me to pretend to be happy. You know, it took me until the age of fifty to tell the truth about what I want. I'm way past pretending things are okay when they're not. I just can't do it well anymore. But I'm not willing to lose Jack."

Helen's determination was courageous, because the consequences were so disappointing. Sometimes the lie does seem easier, but here's the reality check: She doesn't have him and probably never will. That's a lie, too.

Exercise 1: YOUR INNER DOWRY

In certain cultures, the dowry is the price paid in money or goods by a bride's family to permit her marriage into the groom's family. I'd like to suggest a new twist on this archaic custom: a mutual dowry that doesn't involve money or goods but instead offers personal qualities in place of material riches.

• Separately, list the following:

Five positive qualities you are bringing to the marriage:

1.
2.
3.
4.
5.

Exercise continued on next page

Five positive qualities your partner is bringing to the marriage:
1.
2.
3.
4.
5.

• Review each other's lists and have a conversation about what the "items" mean to you. Are there missing items you need to ask for? Are there items on your partner's list that don't represent you, or what you want or desire? Is there anything missing from the list that is tugging at you, that you feel afraid to mention to your partner? There is no time like the present to address these issues. If you're not married, use this list to guide you into making sound choices about the direction of your upcoming marriage. If you are married, this dowry list may explain where some of your conflicts have originated, and you can finally get to the root cause, address the real issues, concerns, misunderstandings, and injuries, and make a plan to readjust your dowry gifting to each other.

MARRIAGE IS FOR GROWN-UPS

You can't have a great marriage if one or both of you is not showing up as a grown-up. You can have a wedding. You can even be married for fifty years. But it won't be a great marriage.

What does it mean to show up as a grown-up?

The desperation people often feel around love is similar to the vulnerable, emotional feelings they have as children, before the part of the brain responsible for evaluation and judgment has developed. The world is full of uncertainty, danger, excitement, and disappointment for a young child, whose constant preoccupation is with getting his needs met. When he wants, he wails. No matter how attentive a parent is, it is impossible to fully satisfy all the needs of the child.

Since a child is unable to meet his own needs, his caretakers become all-powerful. Expressions of praise and disapproval are accepted as fact. A child comes to image himself as the person his parents tell him he is. All of the research supports the fact that early childhood is the period when self-esteem is built up or broken down. It is the time when we either create safe attachments with our caretakers, leading to a sense of emotional and spiritual security; or when the floor beneath our young lives begins to fill itself with cracks of fear, insecurity, and unworthiness.

The imprint of our all-powerful parents can have lasting ramifications, as we will see in the following story.

Lily grew up being told that she was not pretty like her sister, Eleanor. Her parents often said, "Lily is the smart one, and Eleanor is the pretty one." In the early fifties, being smart wasn't valued highly in a young girl, while being pretty afforded one endless admiration and countless social opportunities. Lily definitely felt like she had been given the short end of the stick. Her sister's beauty seemed to afford her so much more attention, including the chance to be loved. In high school, Eleanor had her choice of any boy she liked, while Lily continued to receive straight A's and was rarely asked out on dates.

When Lily was sixteen, Peter, a boy in her class, began to take an interest in her. When he told Lily he thought she was pretty, she was in heaven. But with her happiness came a sense of desperation—a fear that she would do something to drive Peter away. Her entire purpose in life quickly became to cater to Peter, including having sex with him. She gave herself to him and allowed him total power over her happiness. When Peter became interested in another girl—one Lily deemed much prettier—Lily was devastated.

Young love is by nature immature, and Lily eventually might have grown up to appreciate that the obsessive nature and inequality of her relationship with Peter did not meet her true needs. Instead, she patterned every future relationship on her first one, so she was constantly on a roller coaster of intense joy followed by immeasurable pain. To this day, thirty years later, Lily is still looking for the relationship that will transform her and make her feel loved and beautiful. Until she deals with the core issue and wound, she will continue to re-create this cycle of rejection and self-punishment, not realizing that its roots are in the early hurtful and debilitating messages from her parents. Only Lily can stop this cycle of suffering and unfulfilling relationships, but it will require her to face the pain of her childhood that set the fertile groundwork for the unworthiness she feels in her adult life. She needs to put an end to the lie that she is not enough.

Romantic love is the only life state that triggers the same intense need for completeness and connectedness that we experience as children. Dr. Harville Hendrix has advanced the premise that we unconsciously choose mates who reflect both the positive and negative qualities of our original caretakers, in order to resolve the unfinished business of our childhood. That's why people so often say "I knew she was the one as soon as I laid eyes on her" or "I felt as if I'd known him all my life."

Childish Love	Mature Love
Your needs feel immediate and desperate.	*You can put your needs in perspective and feel confident that you know how to get them met.*
You view others as extensions of yourself.	*You consider yourself whole just as you are, and you don't rely on another person to make you complete.*
You fear abandonment.	*You are secure and can tolerate feelings of sadness and anxiety without being consumed by them.*
You need constant reinforcement that you are loved.	*You trust that you are loved and don't constantly search for proof.*

Chart continued on next page

Childish Love	Mature Love
You are dependent on others for your physical and emotional needs.	*You can evaluate situations and make judgments based on reality, and find healthy ways to get your needs met.*
You have no control over your emotions, and you are easily humiliated.	*You accept imperfections in yourself and others and are not humiliated and fearful when you make mistakes.*
You crave certainty.	*You take responsibility for your life but know that you cannot control everything that happens.*
You feel you don't exist outside your loved one's presence.	*You are complete in yourself.*
You live in the moment.	*You plan for the future while living in the moment, having learned from the past.*
You see yourself as the center of the universe.	*You have the capacity for empathy, remorse, and change.*
You fear change and resist stretching yourself.	*You know that stretching outside of your comfort zone is good for you and essential for your overall well-being.*
You will do anything not to lose your relationship, including losing yourself.	*You can accept loss, but never of yourself.*

This familiarity is understandable. When I counsel couples, I sometimes ask, "Where did you learn to speak English?" And they'll reply, "At home," as they silently wonder, what a strange question. And I'll say, "Where did you learn to express love or anger or be silent?" The lightbulb goes off as they realize what I'm getting at, then they reply, "At home."

We are seeking a perfect state of acceptance and safety and are unconsciously drawn to the mate who matches those longings. These strong feelings can block out rational thought. Like children, we are unable to evaluate whether our love interest possesses the qualities to be a good partner.

When the heady cocktail of chemicals that produces strong passion begins to fade, it is not uncommon for partners to become disillusioned with each other, often despising the very qualities they once loved and admired. This is the beginning of the power struggle, and it looks something like this:

"I loved her for her generosity . . . *now* I hate it that she's always running off to take care of other people."
"I loved that he was so quiet and serious . . . *now* I want him to be more talkative when we're around friends and lighten up."
"I loved how professionally accomplished she was . . . *now* I wish she were more domestic and not such a workaholic."
"I was touched by how loving he was toward his mother . . . *now* I wish he wouldn't call her so much."
"She always looked fantastic . . . *now* I wish she wouldn't spend so much money and time on clothes and cosmetics."
"He was so romantic and a wonderful lover . . . *now* I wish he'd stop pushing the issue of sex."
"I loved the way she spoke her mind . . . *now* I wish she'd just keep her complaints to herself."
"I loved that he was so spiritual . . . *now* I wish he'd try to earn more money so we could have a bigger house."
"I loved that she was so willing to share her feelings . . . *now* I wish she'd keep most of them to herself; she's draining me."

The first statement is made under the influence of the love cocktail. The second comes after the high has worn off and your unresolved issues from childhood have popped back into the forefront. Both the infatuation and the power struggle have their sources in unfinished business from childhood. Although infatuation feels like acceptance, it's more about the infatuated person trying to get his or her needs met than it is about the object of infatuation.

Being a grown-up means being able to appreciate that what we may initially be attracted to in a partner doesn't always translate into what we wish to live with for the rest of our lives. We may believe we love others for the qualities that attracted us to them, but often we grow tired of those very things. Mature love requires a deeper sense of who we are and who we're marrying.

Showing up means not just for the wedding but for the marriage. Here's a repeated theme in counseling: A couple will come in after the first year, and she'll be upset that her husband forgot their anniversary. But in exploring further, she'll discover that he didn't just forget their anniversary. He forgot their marriage, and that was the true source of her unhappiness. Or he remembered their anniversary in a big way, with flowers and jewelry, but he wasn't there the rest of the year. The message: Once a year is all you get.

I believe that most marriages can work if people will show up and be committed to growing up. You can stand at the altar and tell the truth about what you're intending, and you can continue to tell the truth over the course of your marriage.

Exercise 2: ARE YOU A GROWN-UP?

Do you struggle to look at life and romance through a grown-up lens? Take the following quick quiz to find out if you're ready for mature love.

1. When my partner is away, I feel insecure or uncertain of his/her devotion.   Yes ☐ No ☐

Exercise continued on next page

2. I am hurt and humiliated when my partner does not respond to my sexual overtures. Yes ❑ No ❑

3. If I don't feel excited to see my partner, something is wrong with our relationship. Yes ❑ No ❑

4. I need to hear my partner say "I love you" in order to feel loved. Yes ❑ No ❑

5. My needs and wishes should always be more important to my partner than the needs and wishes of others. Yes ❑ No ❑

6. I deserve a partner who will always try to make me happy. Yes ❑ No ❑

7. My partner is an extension of myself. Yes ❑ No ❑

8. I'll do almost anything to avoid having an argument with my partner. Yes ❑ No ❑

9. Conflict is damaging to a relationship. Yes ❑ No ❑

10. Marriage means that two individuals have merged to become one entity. Yes ❑ No ❑

EVALUATION: Each "yes" answer involves a fantasy ideal that you hold about love and marriage. These fantasies seem like wonderful ideals, but they are actually remnants of childhood insecurities.

SHOW UP AS A GROWN-UP

Recently, I was watching the news in the wake of severe flooding in the Northeast. A reporter was interviewing a wedding party stranded on the front porch of a reception hall, waiting for rescue. As water swirled up around them, drenching their expensive shoes and mud-dying the hem of the bride's beautiful gown, they were laughing. They'd been thrown a huge curve on their big day. The reception, which they'd been planning for a year, had been ruined. And they were laughing! The bride told the reporter, "Our marriage is start-ing off as an adventure."

Something makes me think this couple will be okay. They un-derstood that the universe throws curves, and they took the storm in stride. Contrast their attitude with the following couple. The bride and groom weren't religious, but he was Jewish, and some of his relatives were observant. Her choice of menu for the wedding dinner included three main courses, one of them loin of pork. When he told her that this would be offensive to his relatives, she didn't get it. "What's the problem? They have a choice of three en-trées," she said. "They can have the chicken or the fish. Big deal."

"It's going to upset them to even see pork on the menu," he in-sisted. "My mother will be humiliated. It'll create unnecessary *tsur-ris*. I'll be in deep trouble."

"*Tsurris, schmurris*," she scoffed.

The pork discussion became a major point of contention be-tween them. Her attitude was "It's my day. I deserve to have exactly what I want." She might as well have been five years old. It was definitely not the behavior of a grown-up. Where was her compas-sion and understanding for the man she was about to pledge her devotion to? If this was happening before the wedding, you can only imagine what was to follow for this couple. Sad to say, these major rifts and red flags come up for couples all the time, and they are dismissed as insignificant annoyances when they are actually the warning signs that deep discussions are needed before they tie the knot.

Sometimes people can speak the truth in vows, but they're un-able to *receive* the truth because they don't trust their partner. They know he or she may believe the words in the moment but be unable to live them.

Ask yourself: Are you a guest at your wedding or a full partici-pant? Marriage doesn't happen *to* you. It happens *through* you.

Exercise 3: REPACK YOUR HOPE CHEST

Hope chests are part of a very long-standing tradition. They're usually filled with fine linens and other goods the bride "hopes" to bring to her marriage. Today's hope chest is different. It acknowledges that hope without action is like a feather on the wind. It is meaningless. So your hope chest must also be packed with actions—the intentional practices that will give substance to your hopes. Remember, you can have all the hope and faith in the world, but without action it is useless, and often creates deep frustration and despair. Repack your hope chest every year, every five years, or whenever you feel the need to refresh your intentions. *Intention* is an important word. It is not good enough to have good relationship intentions if they are not backed up with concrete actions, and these actions must be behaviors that you have learned are valued by your partner. You will get into trouble if you decide that you know how to love your partner without finding out in clear and quantifiable terms what being loved means to your partner.

Three

"IF YOU HAVE ONLY ONE SMILE IN
YOU, GIVE IT TO THE PEOPLE YOU
LOVE. DON'T BE SURLY AT HOME,
THEN GO OUT IN THE STREET AND
START GRINNING 'GOOD MORNING'
AT TOTAL STRANGERS."
—*Maya Angelou*

To Love, Honor, and Cherish

The vow to love, honor, and cherish is the central tenet, the keynote, of the entire wedding ceremony. What an incredible promise! But precisely what do these noble words signify? Do we really mean:

> *"I'll love you as long as you behave in a lovable manner . . . I'll honor you by placing you on a pedestal, then blame you when you tumble off . . . I'll cherish you as long as my heart goes pitter-patter whenever I see you . . . I'll promise to love you unconditionally— until you give me a reason not to . . . I'll accept you for who you are but secretly try to change the parts of you I don't like . . . And I'll always want the best for you, as long as it's good for me, too."*

Let's be clear: "Love, honor, and cherish" may be the most loaded threesome in the English language. Just speaking the words triggers intense emotional reactions. Their potency cannot be overstated. But what does this vow mean in everyday terms? What are we promising each other?

When I've asked couples to clearly tell me what these vows mean to them, their replies are usually vague. These are some of the more common responses:

Love . . .
 "To feel passion for him."
 "Being faithful in body and soul."
 "To adore her."
Honor . . .
 "To admire him."
 "Putting her first."
 "Seeing how special he is."
Cherish . . .
 "Saying 'I love you.'"
 "Making him the center of my life."
 "To hold her close."

These are lovely sentiments, but you can't visualize them. You can't put a practical spin on them. You can't touch them. They seem removed from ordinary life, like precious artifacts you keep on a shelf. And that's the problem. It's all too precious and abstract. How do we make these vows real? How do we love, honor, and cherish someone actively?

I'd like to suggest a new way of looking at these vows—not as static elements or feelings but as dynamically present realities in your relationship. In this new definition:

LOVE is the commitment you make to be present in the marriage. That means being there for each other every day, even when life intrudes and you'd prefer to be somewhere else with someone else.

HONOR is acknowledging and respecting each other as you are, and not harboring intentions of bending the other to your will.

CHERISH is the way you express your love, respect, and compassion in your everyday life. Cherish involves action—the tangible tokens of your regard and the requests you say yes to, the truths you tell and live.

I MAKE A COMMITMENT (*LOVE*) TO
ACKNOWLEDGE YOU AS YOU ARE (*HONOR*) AND TO PERFORM THE ACTIONS
THAT ENHANCE YOUR LIFE AND OUR CONNECTION (*CHERISH*)

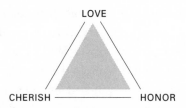

Imagine a triangle, with LOVE at the top, HONOR at the bottom right, and CHERISH at the bottom left. You need all three to keep the triangle in balance.

You cannot LOVE and CHERISH another person if you don't acknowledge him or her for who he or she really is (HONOR)—that is, if you ignore his or her needs, idealize him or her, or think only of trying to change him or her.

You cannot HONOR and CHERISH another person if you haven't made a commitment (LOVE) to be his or her partner—that is, if you stay single within the relationship, always insist on being right, or threaten separation or divorce whenever there's an argument.

You cannot LOVE and HONOR another person if you don't express your commitment and respect in action (CHERISH)—that is, if you are unwilling to perform the daily gestures that enhance your partner's life.

Your vows are not the words you *say*, they are the intentions you *live* in your life together.

On their tenth wedding anniversary, Don presented Melanie with a vase containing ten long-stemmed champagne-colored roses with a card that read, "Thank you for putting up with me for ten years." Melanie stared at that card for a long time, wondering if her gift on their twentieth anniversary would be twenty roses and a card that read, "Thank you for putting up with me for twenty years."

She told me later, "I knew I didn't want a marriage like that. And I knew that I didn't want to teach my daughter that a marriage based on 'putting up' with someone was acceptable."

To love, honor, and cherish may be the work of your marriage, but it is not the *chore* of your marriage. It is not a bouquet of flowers every ten years, nor is it flowery words every day.

"I love you" were easy words for Will to say, and his romantic flair is what attracted Janice to him in the first place. She grew up in a home where affection was pinched like pennies, and she loved Will's expansiveness. He started every day by telling her he loved her. He'd call from work to say, "Have I told you how much I love you today?" And when Janice found out two years into their marriage that Will was having an affair, he said, "It doesn't mean I don't love you."

Love is a commitment to the other, and it lives in the present. A woman in my practice often spoke of her husband's great unrealized potential, something only she could see. She felt powerful in her love for him. He used to tell her, "You believe in me more than I believe in myself." She thought she could love him into changing. She thought she could create someone magnificent from the flawed and complacent man she'd married. She was disappointed when her love didn't bear fruit, but it wasn't love after all.

WRITE A FRESH SCRIPT

Does your relationship feel like a scene from the movie *Groundhog Day*? You may remember the storyline: Actor Bill Murray plays a man forced to relive the worst day of his life over and over again. It's a terrible nightmare. Yet how many couples live out their own personal version of this nightmare, always arguing about the same things, always reacting to the same toxic triggers, never resolving their deepest, most basic conflicts?

It is impossible to truly live the vow to love, honor, and cherish each other if you remain locked in the same old arguments. When you find yourself fighting over the same issues again and again, without ever resolving them, it can drive you crazy. It can lead you to despair. It's a sad moment when you realize that the two of you will never reach an agreement or an understanding that allows you to grow and move forward together. The underlying issues are so important, but you never get to them because you're stuck in the blaming.

Do the following dialogues sound familiar?

SHE: Why don't you ever stand up for me?
HE: You should know better than to get into it with my mother.
SHE: I might as well be alone.
HE: Whose fault is that?
SHE: Fine. I'm outta here.

HE: What do you mean I embarrass you?
SHE: Look at the way you're dressed.
HE: I can never be good enough for you, can I?
SHE: I'm just asking you to put on a tie.
HE: If it means so much to you, you should have chosen one of those country-club jerks your father wanted you to marry.

When the old conflicts turn your marriage into a scene from *Groundhog Day*, it's time to write a new script—one that enables you to listen and respond without the typical knee-jerk reactions that only ratchet up the conflict.

I use a variation of Dr. Harville Hendrix's dialogue to help couples move beyond intractable positions. This is a concrete step that you can take when your horns are locked. It's effective because it gets you out of self-absorption. I know it's hard work, but there is no way to create a strong and respectful love bond without being able to see and hear your partner. It's a three-step process:

Step 1: Mirroring: "Am I hearing you correctly?"
Step 2: Validation: "You make sense to me."
Step 3: Empathy: "From what you just shared, I can imagine how you feel."

Let's explore this method, using as an example a couple I counseled in my practice. Every time Brad and Carol drove anywhere, the same drama occurred. Behind the wheel, Brad was transformed into an angry, aggressive person—honking, swerving in and out of lanes, shouting at other drivers, speeding. At traffic lights, he always maneuvered their car into the right of way, causing near-accidents. Carol huddled in the passenger seat, clutching the door and growing increasingly fearful. She alternately cringed, grimaced, shrieked, and begged Brad to slow down.

Brad thought Carol was being hysterical. "I have never been in an accident," he said. "This is just the way I drive. Carol makes a big deal out of it, but I know what I'm doing. If anything, her crying and carrying on distract me and make things more dangerous. She should just learn to relax."

Brad and Carol had been fighting about Brad's driving for years. The script was well worn, always the same: Brad drove, Carol screamed, Brad got angry, Carol cried. Nobody won, and each time this occurred, it chipped away at the core of the relationship and created less and less emotional safety between them. True intimacy is impossible in the face of fear—emotional, physical, or sexual. Each encounter of disrespect for your partner creates a lack of security, which breeds fear. Fear is a passion and intimacy killer. Fear of your partner and healthy, abiding love cannot live side by side. If you want to have a happy marriage, the safety and security of your partner must be priorities to you.

Setting aside the question of whether Brad's driving mode was unsafe, I suggested to Brad and Carol that they toss out the old script and try an exercise.

They were willing to engage in the three-step dialogue exercise, beginning with mirroring. Mirroring forces you to pay attention to what your partner is actually saying. Often people are in one of two modes. They're either talking or waiting to talk. If it's an old conflict, they're thinking, *I know what you're going to say.* They have their arguments all lined up. They're not listening.

I asked Brad and Carol to sit facing each other. "Carol, tell Brad how you feel. Just express your own feelings in a direct way."

CAROL: When I'm riding with you, I feel sick to my stomach with fear when you go over the speed limit and swerve in and out of lanes. I don't trust you to keep me safe.

At this point, Brad broke in, saying, "I've never been in an accident." His automatic reaction was a replay of the fight they'd had many times. Brad was not listening to Carol; instead, he immediately began defending his position. In this moment, all he could hear or see was himself. Self-absorption, a way of living in the world where you are not able to see another person because your needs dominate and propel everything, is one of the biggest reasons why marriages and intimate partnerships don't work. I explained that this exercise was about *active listening*, not arguing. "Brad," I said, "let's make sure you really heard what Carol was saying. Paraphrase her words back to her, beginning with 'If I hear you correctly . . . ' "

BRAD: If I hear you correctly, you're saying that you are afraid to ride with me because you don't trust me not to kill us both in some horrible accident, and you resent me for this.

I turned to Carol. "Is that accurate?"

"He got part of it right," she said.

"Okay," I said, "tell him what he understood correctly and what part was off."

"He got the part about how scared I was, but I never said I resented him," she replied, looking at Brad, perplexed.

I was curious about what Brad was playing out in this dialogue. Who was he seeing when he looked at Carol? Where did the idea of resentment come from? Who in his past life did he have to so forcefully assert himself with in order to be heard?

The second step of the exercise is validation. "The question for you, Brad, is whether you understand that a person in Carol's position might reasonably have this fear. Does it make sense to you?"

"I think she overreacts," Brad said. It was clear to me and to Carol that Brad still felt defensive about his position. It was their relationship dance, played year in and year out, and they were moving to different tunes.

"But is it possible that riding in a car with you might make someone nervous or upset?" I asked.

Brad and Carol both laughed, and Brad said, "I guess so. My mother won't ride with me."

"Okay," I said. "Now, remember, we're not here to judge your driving. Just to listen to each other. Do you understand that Carol's feelings make sense?"

"Yes."

The final step, empathy, is the most difficult one for some people, because we aren't often asked to put ourselves in another person's shoes. I always tell people, "Empathy requires you to be temporarily egoless. Don't worry, you can put your ego back on in a few minutes." I asked Brad, "Can you recall a situation when you felt physical danger?"

Brad recounted an incident from the previous summer. He'd been out sailing with a friend when a storm hit suddenly. "It was the scariest forty minutes of my life," he said. "We almost went down."

"Imagine, Brad. That's the way Carol feels every time she rides with you," I said.

Brad was shocked. "Oh, that's not what I want," he said to Carol. "I'd never want you to be scared that way."

Although Carol had been telling Brad for years that she was afraid to ride with him, he didn't really *hear* her until he could experience empathy. It not only created more intimacy in their marriage, but Brad became a husband and father full of love, life, and compassion—and a person *he* liked better.

CHERISH IS ACTION

Cherish is action. It is not *wishing*. It is not *trying*. It is doing. People often say "I just want to be happy." Or "I want to make my marriage work." They create the illusion of action by saying they're trying. When you cherish each other, you are interested in meeting each other's needs. It's a balancing act of give and take that many couples struggle with. Few of us had this type of respect and equality modeled for us in our childhoods, even those who were fortunate enough to come from intact and loving families.

Another common refrain is that marriage is about compromise, but what people seem to usually mean is either "You bend to accommodate me" or "I'll bend to accommodate you." For most couples I've worked with, there is a definite sense that the system is unfair. In this hierarchy of needs, one person's comfort always seems to matter more than the other person's comfort. I call it the One Up–One Down dance. Over time, it's the kiss of death to a marriage. The One Up–One Down dance drains all forms of safety, honor, and respect out of the relationship and sets up the partners as adversaries. Even when the issues seem minor and the behavior feels benevolent, inequality is damaging.

I was having dinner with friends, and one of them was explaining her ongoing battle with climate controls. Her home was like a refrigerator. During the winter, her husband insisted on having a window open in the bedroom, and even on the coldest days, he refused to set the thermostat above 65 degrees. In the summer, he insisted that the air-conditioning be kept at its lowest setting. She was freezing. Literally.

A woman at the table laughed, saying, "Tell me about it. All men are like that with the temperature."

I had a different response. I said, "Wait a minute. You're supposed to freeze for the rest of your life just because *men are like that?*"

We are so quick to write off our partners because of stereotypes, past experiences, or the messages we were taught and that others reinforce. Because of this ingrained image of the opposite sex, we make up stories about what is possible and what is not without ever testing out our assumption, or looking to see what role we play in keeping the outcome the "same old, same old."

In marriage, you have a right to get your needs met, and so does your partner. This means asking for what you need with the expectation that your partner will have an interest in wanting you to get it—and vice versa. If you've never learned to ask for what you need, or have never been conscious enough of your needs to identify them, you will struggle mightily with this issue. Many people learn from the time they're children that their needs are not going to be met, that their expressed needs are a burden or unrealistic. When they express their needs, they are told they're being whiny and self-ish, or that they are being bad or unreasonably demanding. They feel ashamed to have to ask for what they want.

I have a great deal of compassion for those of you who are struggling with this issue because, as I have mentioned, I grew up in a family where the One Up–One Down mode was perfected. My father was a godlike figure, and we revolved around him like planets circling the sun. My father was also at the forefront of important social movements. I grew up in a home that marched for equality with Dr. Martin Luther King, Jr., and embraced the words of Gandhi. These were powerful and positive ideals that shaped me in life. However, in the midst of all the messages about giving and caring, there were few messages about how to self-protect. We were taught to have compassion for others, even at our own expense, which meant we could easily be harmed while feeling bad for the person who harmed us. We were taught that if people were mean, they were hurting inside, and while that may have been true, it didn't leave room for us to remove ourselves from their meanness. There were no messages about protecting ourselves, about saying no. Relationship reciprocity and boundaries were not taught or practiced. No one seemed to know how to master these tough but learnable skills. As a result, I became very good at taking lemons and making lemonade. It would not have occurred to me to say, "This is too sour, I'll pass." This excessive generosity caused me problems in my adult relationships, until I learned that *I* mattered, too.

Goodness without boundaries makes victims. Women in particular are overly focused on being good. You can't say yes without being able to say no. The challenge for women is to fight centuries of being socialized to please.

Let me state this very clearly: It is NOT a solution to just decide that you *don't* need what you *do* need. Not only does it fail miserably, but in the process, you dishonor yourself and the viability of your own needs. You sell yourself and your partner short by denying the opportunity to stretch and grow into your better selves. If you aren't a self, you're missing half of what you need in a healthy relationship.

Arlene was unhappy in her marriage, but she couldn't articulate the problem. She couldn't figure out why she felt so frustrated and discontented. "Carl and I never fight," she said. I could tell that it was a point of pride for her. It also quickly became clear that she pushed her personal mute button whenever a disagreement threatened to erupt between them.

Arlene didn't want to be one of those "high-maintenance girls." She figured there were plenty of other women waiting in the wings who wouldn't require as much attention as she did. She was afraid that if she spoke up for herself, made any demands, she might lose Carl. But what was the price of her silence? She stayed married by staying on guard. She swallowed her words, her voice, and her truth.

I asked Arlene why she thought her husband's needs were the only ones that counted. She told me that she had been brought up that way.

Arlene had grown up in a family where being a "good girl" was given a high value. "I was a Goody Two-Shoes," she admitted, "and that's the way I was raised. You won approval by being supremely considerate and agreeable. All the women in my family were like that. My grandmother's motto was 'Never say a cross word.' I don't think I ever saw her without a smile on her face. She'd tell me, 'Don't frown, darling. It will cause wrinkles in your forehead.'"

As a result of her upbringing, Arlene avoided conflict like the plague. She'd learned that asking for what she needed got her into trouble and upset people. It seemed much easier to go along with what others wanted and keep the peace. Carl had chosen the perfect partner for smooth sailing. He got what he wanted (not what he *needed*) and never heard a harsh word directed at him by his loving wife. But it was destroying her soul and their marriage.

Silence wasn't golden in this marriage; it was deadly. Both Carl and Arlene had created an environment that was bound to negatively impact their sense of connection and intimacy. What in their pasts made this type of arrangement appealing to them? On the surface, both were comfortable with an arrangement of placating and one-sided accommodation. What burdens was Carl carrying that made him comfortable with a mute wife? Where in his history had words overpowered him or someone he cared for? And where had Arlene learned the survival skill of going along to keep the peace? A healthy relationship stretches us into growing the areas that are emotionally, spiritually, and physically underdeveloped.

General	Specific
I need you to be more thoughtful.	*It would mean a lot to me if you would call me when you're going to be late coming home from work.*
I need affection.	*I would appreciate it if once this week you would greet me with a kiss when you come in the door.*
I need space.	*I need to have fifteen minutes alone when I come home from work to change clothes and shift gears. Then I will have more to offer to you and the kids.*
I need you to pay more attention to me.	*I'm asking that we have one evening a week when the TV is off and we can spend quality time together.*
I need you to be considerate of my feelings.	*I would feel respected if you did not joke that I have PMS when I am upset.*

HOW TO ASK FOR WHAT YOU NEED

We like to think that our most intimate partner—the one who knows us best—can read our mind. How many times do we say, "If you really knew me, you'd know what I want"? But none of us are mind readers, no matter how great our love. We need to ask. It's so simple yet so difficult.

I encourage couples to learn to ask for what they need, using three guidelines that help assure a satisfying response:

1. Think small. A little bit at a time. Something concrete and doable.

2. Think specific. Ask for exactly what you need.

3. Think positive. Don't threaten or accuse. Make having your needs met beneficial for both of you.

Exercise 1: **MAKE A REQUEST**

Write down three requests you can make of your partner, keeping them small and specific. For example, you might make this request: "When my parents come to visit us from out of town, I would like for you to sit with me when they first arrive and spend time greeting them."

This seems like a specific request, but it can still be misinterpreted. Make it even more specific: "When my parents come to visit us from out of town, I would like for you to join us for an hour when they first arrive, visiting and helping them get settled." Strive to make your requests as concrete as possible. As the saying goes, the devil is in the details. It's the fine print of our lives that trips us up.

Practice asking and responding. You'll get the hang of it and be glad you did. One couple I know has a "request night" once a week. Just knowing you can rely on having a simple need met has a transformational effect. Being cherished in action leads to *feeling* cherished, and that leads to deepening your intimate connections.

HONOR THE ONE YOU'RE WITH

When you vow to honor your partner, you are promising two things: first, that you will see the other person clearly for who he or she is; second, that you will respect that person. A man I know told of being at his new in-laws' house, and his mother-in-law kept calling him by his wife's first husband's name. "It was embarrassing," he said. "I kept looking over at my wife, waiting for her to say, 'Mother, his name is John, not Steve.' Instead, she laughed and said, 'Oh, Mom, you're so cute.' I didn't think it was cute at all, but I kept my mouth shut."

You can't honor a person who has to live a lie to get along with you. You can't honor a person who doesn't actually exist except in your fantasy. But this is where many lies at the altar occur.

A couple came to see me. They were in real pain and on the verge of a divorce. I wasn't sure I would be able to help them, because their dispute was centered on their core values. Jacki and Michael had been married for six years, and it was immediately apparent that they loved each other very much. The disagreement that was tearing them apart was classic. Jacki desperately wanted to have a child, and Michael absolutely did not want a child.

"We talked about this seriously and at length before we married," Michael said defensively. "There was nothing vague or unspoken at all. I was honest with Jacki. I didn't want to have children, and if we were going to get married, she would have to accept that. She agreed. She knows how much I love her. Our marriage has been wonderful. Now, after we've been together for six years, she tells me that she has to have a child or her life will feel empty and she'll be unfulfilled. So now we're constantly arguing about something that I thought was clearly resolved."

Jacki admitted that everything Michael said was true. "But people change," she said. "I didn't know I was going to feel this way then. And I didn't know for sure when we got married that he really meant he didn't want children." Jacki was miserable. She wiped tears from her eyes as she spoke.

"I'm not here to judge you," I said to Jacki, "but let me make sure I understand you correctly. When you agreed before you married that you wouldn't have children, you were thinking that there was still some wiggle room?"

She nodded. "Yes. I didn't want to lose Michael. I thought he'd change his mind someday. We have a great marriage. And I think he'd make such a great daddy."

Jacki had stood at the altar and vowed to honor Michael, but she wasn't accepting him for the man he had told her he was. When she looked at him, she saw a daddy, the father of her future children, even though he had made it absolutely clear to her that he had no intention of being that person. And while it's true that some people who are resistant to having children change their minds once they feel secure in their marriages and awaken to new feelings, you should never make a vow in anticipation of the other person changing his or her mind about issues vital to both of you.

"Jacki lied," I said to Michael. "She lied to herself and she lied to you. But I suspect that you were lying a little bit, too. There must have been some indication that Jacki might want children someday. She was agreeing to your ultimatum somewhat against her will, because she loved you and wanted to spend the rest of her life with you. You chose to accept her agreement with your desires at face value, hoping the subject would never come up again."

Michael sighed. "I guess that maybe I had some doubts," he said.

Michael and Jacki had engaged in a mutual deception over a core value, and the consequences were potentially catastrophic. They were in a real bind. The only way for them to resolve this seemingly impossible standoff was to look into the past and sort out where the strains of denial and deceit had their roots. They were surprised when I suggested that in the first instance the issue wasn't about whether or not to have a child. "You need to know who *you* are first," I said. "You're viewing this as an external debate, one that is completely outside of yourselves. You each have strong positions, but you don't even know why."

When we fly off the handle, or dig our heels into the cement of an issue, I call this being emotionally hijacked. It is as if some unknown terrorist has entered our heads and hearts, and has invaded us and taken over the cockpit of our rational thinking selves. I have asked people, "What were you thinking when you said that you would leave your partner before you would ever consider having a child with him?" "What were you thinking when you screamed in your partner's face, cursing at her and calling her every name except a child of God?" "What were you thinking when you gave your partner the silent treatment until you broke him down to get your way?" The answer, when someone is being honest, is usually, "I wasn't thinking." And to this, my response is, "Great, now we are working from the world of truth." Only people who have been emotionally hijacked behave in ways that create fear in their partners. And once fear rules the day, there is no hope of getting either person's needs met. If you learn to manipulate your partner with fear, by threatening infidelity, emotional withdrawal (the silent treatment), or other forms of emotional or physical acting out, you may temporarily get what you want, but in the long run you will lose your partner's trust, respect, and sometimes even their love.

Over many months, we looked back into their childhoods to unearth the wounds they were still holding on to. Michael had been raised in a family of Jehovah's Witnesses. From the time he and his brothers were very young, they had been taken door-to-door in strange neighborhoods to pass out literature and proselytize about their religion. Michael found this exhausting and excruciating. Most people were unreceptive, and often he found the door slammed in his face as he stood trembling on the doorstep. Recalling those experiences, Michael sat in my office with tears streaming down his face. "I vowed I would never bring children into the world who could be destroyed this way," he said.

What was so moving to me was how raw and available those old feelings were to Michael, because at last he felt safe enough to air them. Michael had struggled with his faith for years. There were parts of it that still held great meaning for him, and other parts that he could not reconcile. Marrying outside of his faith was bad enough. To have a child and be forced to grapple with his own unresolved issues while trying to navigate a clearer path for his child just felt too big. Before now, he had been so emotionally hijacked that he'd never been able to discuss this with Jacki.

As Jacki listened, you could have heard a pin drop. I could see some of her closed and blaming positions begin to melt away. She wanted to know her husband deeply, intimately, and passionately, and this was her chance. She didn't blow it by getting into her own self-absorption and hijacked feelings.

Michael equated being a parent with bringing pain. He didn't trust himself to break the cycle, so he decided he would never have children. Once he was able to view his parents' actions as their own, and to reject that legacy for himself, he became less fearful.

"You are free to choose not to have children," I told him. "But your choice needs to grow out of your power, not your fear."

The same was true for Jacki. She had grown up being told that she was not good enough in herself. She needed a marriage and children to fulfill her. Because that belief was so firmly rooted, and so frequently reinforced by society, she had never questioned it. She was stunned to discover that the source of her great desire to have a family with Michael was the terror that she could not exist without it.

For the first time Jacki realized that her desperation and the pressure she placed on Michael was not about having a child to share in this joy with him. It was a response to her mother's admonition that the only way to be good enough was to marry the right man and have a child with him. She had the man, but Jacki still needed a child to fulfill her mother's dreams and win her love and approval. Jacki was unaware that her childhood pain of never being accepted by her mother had filtered into her marriage with a man who loved and accepted her fully for who she was. By not recognizing Michael's goodness and the gift he offered of full acceptance, she was, in effect, objectifying him in the same way that she had been objectified by her mother.

Because their mutual love and respect was strong, Michael and Jacki agreed to work on resolving their fears and growing together. Although they knew it would be difficult, they were exhilarated by the possibility that they could decide their future together—including whether or not they had children—instead of having it decided for them by their childhood wounds.

In the end, what felt impossible became their reality. They fully understood what had been placed on their marital table by their parents, society, and other influences. Jacki was no longer sure that she wanted to have a child, at least not now. First, she needed to sort out her need versus her mother's need—and the extent to which she was just trying to win her mother's acceptance. Michael was willing to consider having a child because he realized that he could and would make healthier choices for his children than his parents had made. He also knew that if Jacki decided she wanted a child it would now be out of a mutuality of love between them. What was once a deal breaker in their relationship became the deal maker. They made a deal to truly love, honor, and cherish each other. This was the real beginning of their marriage vows being lived to their fullest, and the best was yet to come. We had all witnessed the miracle of hard work, two open, vulnerable, and honest hearts, and the humility required to share their sacred stories. This is love in action, and it is what is possible when maturity and compassion are chosen over being right and winning.

Even when the issue is less crucial, conflicts over identity cause problems in marriage.

Kathy's friends jokingly referred to her as "the hostess with the mostest" because she loved to entertain and arrange elaborate festivities, especially for holidays and birthdays. Her husband, Craig, tolerated her passion, for the most part, since it gave Kathy so much pleasure, but he tried to draw the line at his own birthday.

For years before he met Kathy, Craig had chosen to spend his birthday basically alone, doing something enjoyable that allowed time for reflection—hiking, kayaking, or writing in his journal. His family had never made much of birthdays while he was growing up. He didn't like the celebration or the cake, and he thought it was silly to encourage people to spend good money on gifts he didn't want or need.

Kathy couldn't understand why Craig would want to be alone on his birthday. In her family, birthdays were a cause for major celebration, with a cake, candles, many presents, and required attendance by all of the relatives. A big party was the best way she knew to express her love.

The first year they were married, Kathy announced to Craig that she had invited a few people over for his birthday celebration and had planned a special dinner and a cake. This set off an emotional confrontation.

CRAIG: Cancel it, Kathy. You know I don't like parties on my birthday.
KATHY: But I want to do something special for you, honey.
CRAIG: You can do that by leaving me alone.
KATHY: Don't you love me?
CRAIG: Just throw your own party, if it means so much to you, but leave me out of it.

Kathy wanted Craig to feel happy about her plans for his birthday, because they were her way of expressing love. When he rejected her plan, her hypersensitive reaction was "Don't you love me?" She didn't see that her way of doing something special for Craig was really about meeting her own expectations, feeling good about herself, not meeting his expectations and making him feel good. A big celebration was not what he wanted, and Kathy already knew that.

Meanwhile, Craig dug himself a deeper hole in the dispute by insisting that he just wanted to be left alone, turning his preference for a quiet celebration into an explicit rejection of Kathy's desire to give him something special.

Kathy didn't realize it, but in the guise of meeting Craig's needs, she was really meeting her own needs. She was doing it for herself, not for him. She wasn't even seeing him. She knew who he was. She knew he didn't enjoy the same things that she enjoyed.

A more respectful conversation might have gone like this:

KATHY: I want to do something special for you on your birthday. Tell me what you'd like.
CRAIG: I like to spend time alone on my birthday, reflecting on my life. I think I'll take the day off and go hiking. Would you make me one of your famous turkey sandwiches to take along?
KATHY: Sure. And maybe we can have a quiet dinner later.
CRAIG: That sounds perfect.

It was important for Kathy to understand that the need to celebrate Craig in a manner that didn't honor him was her way of trying to hold on to good childhood memories. Kathy's mother had died from Alzheimer's, and her father had recently been diagnosed with it. Trying to re-create happy memories was Kathy's way of avoiding her grief and fear about losing her parents and her life as she once knew it. As Kathy came to understand this, she stopped using Craig to shield her from her pain and grief. And as Craig gained more understanding of Kathy's struggle, he was able to express greater compassion for her losses. While Craig and Kathy continue to live in the world with different social rhythms, the honor, care, and respect they've come to have for each other's unique styles have made the fiber of their marriage remarkably strong and solid.

The ultimate form of disrespect in an intimate relationship is to refuse to see the truth about the person you are committed to. This is especially the case in marriage, because this is where we tend to expose ourselves completely. When you stand before your partner naked and vulnerable and say, "This is who I am," it is devastating to hear him or her say back, "I can't accept you, so I'm going to mold you into somebody better."

What is the answer then? How can we honor our partner and get our individual needs met as well? Commitment requires an openness to chiseling away at the layers of entrenched beliefs you carry around from childhood, in order to create something authentic that belongs to you. So if you have to celebrate a holiday in a certain way because you are determined to re-create childhood images of joy (which may not have been so joyful even then), you can't be a full partner. You must acknowledge that there's another person who needs consideration. Or, if you are emotionally uptight and you say, "That's just the way we are in my family. We're private people," you have to give up that old self-image should it stop working in your marriage.

There are too many people divorced today because they were unable to join their spouses in the present and engage fully in the task of building the future. They are bound by the page of self-stories that reads THE END before the marriage has even begun. Make a commitment to start your marriage on page one.

Exercise 2: DEFINING LOVE IN ACTION

Using the definitions of to LOVE, HONOR, and CHERISH described on page 47, each of you should complete the following statements.

I experience LOVE when you _____.
I experience HONOR when you _____.
I experience being CHERISHED when you _____.

I express LOVE when I _____.
I express HONOR when I _____.
I express that I CHERISH my partner when I _____.

When you have finished filling in the blanks, share your responses with your partner. Discuss what you have learned about each other. What surprised you? Was anything missing that has value? Was anything listed that caused you concern?

This exercise can create a real bond that might not have existed otherwise. Being able to transform vague promises into concrete statements and tangible actions has a healing, invigorating effect on relationships. You may discover that to love, honor, and cherish isn't such a heavy burden, and that you needn't fear these vows will make you disappear as an individual.

Four

Forsaking All Others

Most people believe that the vow to forsake all others means being sexually faithful. But sexual infidelity is only a part of it. The irony is, being sexually exclusive with your partner may be only one of your worries. Those *other* kinds of infidelity usually end up creating as deep a conflict in marriages as sexual infidelity.

When we promise to forsake all others, do we really mean:

> *"Except my family—blood is thicker than marriage—and, of course, my friends (including my ex—we're just friends now, really). Oh, and naturally, my kids from my previous marriage will always come first . . . Sundays are reserved for dinner with my folks . . . and you know what I always say: 'Love me, love my St. Bernard, Toby.'"*

Or you get someone who fervently means it:

> *"We will be joined at the hip and completely fulfilled in each other's company. We will refuse most invitations to social gatherings (and even when we accept, I'll whine and complain the whole time). We will never go on a trip without the other, and we'll always want the same things (I'll tell you precisely what they are).*

And don't be upset if I seem obsessively jealous. It's only because I love you so much."

What's *your* subtext? Under what set of rules do you operate? What are the fears you're harboring? Do you believe that blood is thicker than the water of your vows, that loyalty to your spouse is a betrayal of your family contract? Do you believe that your close friendships will forever stay the same? Vows do not mean that all of your other relationships are finished. Instead, they will have a new position in your life, occupy a different seat at your Marriage Table.

THE MARRIAGE TABLE

When you first fall head over heels in love, the idea of being alone together on a desert island may seem quite appealing. But you'd soon grow bored if that dream were to come true. All relationships exist within a larger community, where they are nurtured and where they mature.

I like to envision the setting of a new relationship as a Marriage Table. This is not an intimate little table for two. Instead, it's more of a banquet table with extra leaves inserted, expanded to fit all of the people who have an influence on the two of you. Some of us have too many leaves, some of us don't have enough leaves. What's the makeup of *your* table?

Imagine you and your spouse sitting together at the center of your Marriage Table, with your guests fanned out on either side. To the groom's right, you may find his parents, grandparents, an uncle or two, various siblings, and their spouses and children. To the bride's left, you'll see a similar collection, larger or smaller depending on the size of her family. On both sides, you'll notice a couple of ghostly figures hovering around. Every family has its dearly departed members whose influence remains strong in the way they act in our own lives. The departed have never really left the table.

Continuing around the table (according to their order of influence), you'll find: children from a previous marriage, the bride's boss, the groom's ex-wife, her college roommate, his oldest buddy, her first boyfriend, their family doctor, their best friends as a couple, various coworkers, a therapist or two, a pastor, a rabbi, an imam, the next-door neighbors, the cat, the dog, and a couple of empty booster seats that can be squeezed in with the arrival of new children. Phew. This is a big table.

At the farthest reaches of the table, sometimes speaking softly and other times loudly dominating the conversation, are the voices from the past—the ones who lifted you up or cut you down—your gender, racial, religious, and social models.

Over time, some of the guests will leave the table. Others will move to different seats, depending on circumstances. New faces will appear. The Marriage Table is a busy, changeable place, like a game of musical chairs.

Occasionally, one of you will look up, notice a new guest, and whisper to your spouse, "Who invited *him*?" You'll find that your life as a couple is inseparably intertwined with those of your guests at the Marriage Table. Your greatest conflicts will involve them, and the success of your marriage will rest in large part on how well you manage those conflicts. Yet there will be times when you'll look at the faces around you and feel supreme joy and gratitude.

WHO'S NUMBER ONE?

We all long for that one special relationship. We all want someone who is on our side, do or die. We long for the one person who will stand up for us and be our absolute ally in the world. That's why marriage holds such a unique place. It's a closer, deeper, more intimate bond than any other. It is often experienced as finding a missing piece of oneself, which is why lovers will say "You complete me" or "You are my soul mate." Lovers speak of being destined to find each other, as if they were separated at birth only to be joyfully reunited as adults.

Such a special intimacy can be powerful and wonderful, but it can also bring to the surface fears of abandonment, which are the buried residue of childhood wounds. Our first experience of life was one of symbiosis. We lived in our mother's womb. Her breath was as ours, and her organs sustained and nourished us. The day of our birth is also a day of traumatic separation from our cocoon of safety. As a comedian once joked, "No wonder babies cry when they're pulled from their mother's womb. They'll never have it so good again."

The total vulnerability of young life cements the need for this closeness. Infants and young children experience a primal fear of abandonment because they are completely unable to take care of themselves. Ideally, a child will gradually learn to separate and make judgments that are not purely emotional or based on fear. However, if home is a dangerous or uncertain place, if the adults are unable to nurture a sense of well-being, and if parents are not attuned to the child's truest needs, the fear of abandonment will be imprinted on the child's brain. This will have an impact on adult life until the unresolved issues are acknowledged, addressed, and resolved.

It isn't only the survivors of childhood trauma who struggle with these fears. Even if you were raised in a loving, nurturing environment and are a reasonably well-adjusted adult, the intensity of romantic love can feel like the symbiosis of the womb and trigger the neediness of early childhood. In my practice, couples often talk about feeling helpless in the face of powerful emotions. They don't understand why sudden surges of anger or disappointment overwhelm them—why a certain look or word from their partner can push the one button that sends them into the orbit of misunderstanding, resentment, and pain.

It's not surprising that these emotions are strongest when a partner's loyalty is in question. When your seatmate at the Marriage Table leaves your side to go sit with his mother, or with her girlfriends, or with his colleagues, it can trigger those early feelings of abandonment.

Jim's eighty-year-old mother was a feisty, independent woman who had lived alone since the death of Jim's father ten years before.

However, after she suffered a minor stroke, Jim knew she could no longer live on her own. "It's clear to me that the only solution is for Mom to come and live with us after she gets out of the rehab center," Jim told his wife, Pamela. Jim's words sent Pamela into a tailspin of anger and resentment. They were tantamount to throwing down a gauntlet. She could barely tolerate his mother at a distance. How could Jim expect her to live with the woman? Their conversation was explosive:

PAMELA: No way. If she moves in, I move out.

JIM: She's a sick old woman. We have a responsibility to take care of her.

PAMELA: It's not my responsibility. You obviously don't care that it would make *me* sick to have her living in my house.

JIM: How can you be so heartless?

PAMELA: Heartless? How dare you! I guess I know where I stand.

By the time this couple came to me, they were barely speaking. The air was electric with the explosive fuel of their anger, hurt, and blame, each certain that he or she was right and the other was selfish and wrong.

Jim acknowledged that his mother could be difficult, but as an only child, he believed he was fully responsible for her care. When his father was alive, he didn't worry, but now he felt he had to step up to the plate. "What else can I do?" he asked.

Pamela was furious that Jim had presented her a unilateral decision, without any consideration for her feelings. She felt betrayed that he would insist on an arrangement he knew would make her miserable. She'd often told Jim how burdened she'd felt as a child, being the oldest daughter in a large family. She'd felt used by her mother as a caretaker for her younger siblings, and that had always bothered her. Now she was preparing to do what *she* wanted for the first time in her life, and he was slamming the door on her freedom.

How could they break this impasse? "It seems hopeless," Jim said dejectedly.

"I agree," I said. "It *is* hopeless as long as you treat the discussion as a debate in which one of you expects to be declared the winner. Let me give you an alternative image. Rather than thinking of your conflict as a debate, try thinking of it as a problem-solving discussion between two people who are committed to taking care of each other and themselves." Respect and compassion for your partner—yes, even in the face of an impasse—are essential for true repair to begin.

When couples fight, instead of listening to each other, they're usually preparing their next argument. They are either talking or waiting to talk, creating walls of isolation and fury in the relationship. As the fight escalates, it veers off course, derailing into accusations and recriminations that are close to the angry wail of an infant:

HE: *Waaaah!*
SHE: *Waaah! Waaah!*
HE: *Waaaaaaaaaah!*

It's pretty hard to solve problems this way. The first step in having an effective conversation is to listen with love. That means being able to hear what your partner is saying.

I asked Pamela to tell Jim how she felt, and he was to empathically listen to her words. To listen with empathy means putting aside your own agenda and defensiveness for the moment, and opening your heart and mind to feelings other than your own. This is a sign of commitment and maturity. When you listen with empathy, you create an atmosphere of safety, respect, and love.

PAMELA: When you announced that your mother had to
move in with us, I was hurt that you didn't
consider my feelings. I've spent all these years raising
the kids, and now that I finally have some time for
myself, I'm going to end up being stuck in the house
with your mother, who you know I can only take in

very small doses. And you seem to think it's okay if
I'm unhappy.

When Pamela had stopped speaking, I turned to Jim. "Jim," I said, "let's make sure you really heard what Pamela was saying. Paraphrase her words back to her, beginning, 'If I hear you correctly, you're saying . . .'" Just saying the words sheds some of the arrogance of thinking we know what our partner is going to say. It raises the possibility that we could be missing the boat and not getting the essence of what's being said. It brings to the surface the all-too-common reality that we haven't heard what our partner said. Too often we're responding to the voices in our own heads.

JIM: If I hear you correctly, you're saying that you were hurt when I said my mother was moving in, because I wasn't thinking about how you'd feel. And you're afraid you'll be stuck in the house with Mom and it will make you miserable. Did I get that right?

Pamela nodded her agreement. "Now, Jim," I continued, "knowing Pam's issues about being used in her childhood, do her feelings make sense to you?"

"Yeah, they do. I know it would be hard for her. Besides, she and my mom don't really see eye-to-eye on most things," Jim said sheepishly.

"Don't tell me," I said. "Look at Pamela and speak your words of understanding to her." And Jim did that—beautifully, I might add.

"So, how do you imagine Pamela feels?" I asked.

"Trapped, cornered, disrespected, scared, hurt," he replied. "Angry, too."

"Ask Pamela if those are the feelings she's burdened by." He did.

Pamela hung her head and quietly wept, murmuring, "Yes, those are the feelings."

What were Pamela's tears about? She cried because she felt the care, honor, and respect from Jim that she'd never received in childhood. This unmet need was still demanding to be addressed in her adult life and relationships.

The ability to express empathy is an incredible tool in a couple's dialogue. It can move them from feeling miles apart to being in the same room, where they can actually communicate and create bridges of intimate connections where only stone walls existed before.

Next we reversed the process, with Jim expressing his feelings and Pamela listening with an empathic, open, and curious heart.

JIM: When Dad was dying, he kept begging me to take care of Mom. He was so worried about her. I told him I would, and he made me promise over and over. I'm the only one she has. I don't know what else to do.

PAMELA: I hear you saying that you promised your dad you'd take care of your mom, and you don't know any other way than to bring her to live with us.

By the time Pamela had validated Jim's feelings and expressed empathy, the mood in the room had been transformed from blaming and critical to soft, understanding, and caring. The exercise had restored their feelings of closeness. The anger had dissolved. Now they were ready to work on solving the problem, starting from the place of mutual concern for Jim's mother and a deep sense of caring and devotion for each other. The loyalty lines of devotion first to each other were clearly established. The issue for Jim was the burden he had carried all his life as an only child, and that his father had reinforced on his deathbed: *Look after your mother at all costs, including sacrificing yourself and your life.*

As Jim and Pamela reviewed the options, they realized there was a third person who had a say in the outcome—Jim's mother. What would she want? Knowing that her preference would be to remain independent, they decided to meet with the counselors at the rehab center and find out what was available in home nursing care and assisted living facilities. They also agreed to investigate long-term options should her health decline further. They left my office as a team, committed to working together.

An impossible deadlock had been overcome. Two closed doors had become one open door. The big shift for Jim and Pamela was not in what would ultimately happen to Jim's mother. It was in their conscious choice and committed desire to forsake the isolating force of ego for the mature posture of consideration and collaboration.

LOVE ME, LOVE MY CHILD

Another common conflict that usually gets ignored in marriage preparation arises when one or both partners have children from previous marriages. This is increasingly common. Today over 65 percent of all remarriages involve kids, and there are twenty million stepfamilies in America. People tend to envision their future as a scene from *The Brady Bunch*, in which miraculously, two disparate families, with established loyalties and styles, integrate lovingly into one big happy blended unit.

It's not going to happen. When you bring children into a marriage, it changes the dynamic from the start. You never get a chance to be "we two." This is true even when the children are adults.

Stephen and Laura met in their forties, and it was a second marriage for both of them. Stephen had no children, and Laura had a twenty-three-year-old son, Greg, who was attending college out of state. He graduated a year after they were married and found an entry-level job at a firm back home. Laura was thrilled to have her son living nearby, and she threw herself into helping Greg. She spent a lot of time and money setting up his apartment, even filling his refrigerator with food and doing his laundry. For Laura, this was a labor of love. Stephen saw it differently. Not only did he think Laura was pampering Greg, he resented the amount of time she spent with her son.

Neither Laura nor Stephen realized that this showdown had been hovering in the wings of their placid existence. Since Greg had been away from home for the entire period of their courtship and marriage, Laura and Stephen hadn't discussed the role he would play in their lives. Laura had assumed that if her son came back to the area after college, she would be very involved with him, but she neglected to mention this to Stephen. For his part, Stephen assumed that Greg would be busy doing his thing and would only peripherally affect them. Since Stephen had no children of his own, he didn't think about the subject often. Besides, Stephen had been quite self-sufficient when he was young, and he presumed that Greg would (and should) be the same way. This is one of the biggest ways that couples get into trouble—the fantasy that "we are all the same."

Now Stephen felt like the odd man out, neglected and jealous. He did the one thing guaranteed to provoke Laura's ire. He attacked her son:

STEPHEN: You coddle that spoiled son of yours.
LAURA: Spoiled? You have no right to attack my son.
STEPHEN: Come on, Laura. The kid is twenty-four. He can get along without his mommy.
LAURA: What is *that* supposed to mean?
STEPHEN: I can see if you had to choose between him and me, you'd choose him.
LAURA: [*walking out of the room*] Oh, grow up!
STEPHEN: [*calling after her*] Why don't you just move in with him. Then you'd both be happy.

POW! BANG! It was a verbal slugfest, and both Laura and Stephen came away injured and felt the other was fully at fault.

In my office, I helped them through the mirroring exercise, which had the effect of cleansing the vitriol from the air and allowing them to have a real conversation about Laura's son. In the course of that conversation, each of them uncovered a remarkable truth.

I tried to help Stephen understand why Laura's relationship with her son caused him so much pain. Clearly, the issue wasn't just money, nor was it the time Laura spent with her son. He thought about it for a while and then replied, "My parents taught me to stand on my own two feet. By the time I was Greg's age, I had been supporting myself for years. It wasn't easy, either. I really struggled, but that's part of growing up. I remember once I was practically down to my last buck and I wasn't going to make the rent. I called my folks and asked for a loan—maybe fifty, a hundred dollars, something like that. My dad said, 'Can't help you.'" Stephen grimaced, remembering. "I think he was trying to build my character."

"And you felt?"

Stephen shrugged.

"I imagine you felt alone and scared," I said.

"Yeah." He stared at his hands. "I sure could have used some help."

"It would have been comforting to have their support," I said. "Maybe when you see Laura doing so much for her son, you wish it had been you."

Stephen was shaken by my words. It had never occurred to him to look at it that way. We often choose partners because of some unfinished business from the past. In Laura, Stephen had found the nurturing presence he'd long craved. But when she nurtured her son, it triggered Stephen's old feelings of abandonment. He realized that his distress wasn't directed at Laura or her son but inwardly, at himself. This was what he was running from.

Stephen's revelation touched Laura deeply. It also started her thinking about what kind of parent she had been. "I know I overdo it," she admitted. "Greg doesn't need me to fill his refrigerator. But when he was younger, I was so busy with my career, I didn't always have time to do the things moms should do. I guess I'm trying to make up for it now. I, too, didn't have help when I most needed it, and I never wanted Greg to feel the aloneness that I felt. I covered up many of my feelings of inadequacy as a parent and how let down I felt by my own parents, who loved me but left me on my own, by overcompensating."

"I think you're a wonderful mother," Stephen said. "You've raised a good kid. You don't have anything to prove."

I sat back and looked at Stephen and Laura with admiration. "You are an amazing couple," I said. "You have shared some pretty deep vulnerabilities here today. Can you now see the possibility of resolving this conflict?"

They could and did. Feeling less threatened, Stephen was more open to establishing his own relationship with Greg. Laura saw that she'd gone overboard in an effort to compensate for the times in the past when she wasn't there. She needed to understand and forgive herself for choices she couldn't undo, and see her son as the capable, competent adult he was today.

NEW MAP, NEW RULES

Recently, I counseled a newly married couple. They had never discussed the role that their friends would play in their lives. For the past eight years, Ruth and her best friend, Eileen, had a standing date to meet two Saturday afternoons a month for lunch. Ruth's new husband, Sam, was surprised when Ruth informed him the lunches would continue. "I thought it was a single-girl thing," he said. "I assumed the lunches would stop. I figured you'd hang out with me."

"No way," Ruth replied. "I don't know what made you think that."

So Sam was upset that his wife continued her lunches with her friend Eileen. At the same time, Ruth was annoyed that Sam's buddy Fred felt free to drop by their place unannounced and, as she put it, "never leave." Sam refused to tell Fred that he should call first. "I don't want to make him feel like we don't want him there," he explained.

Welcome to the mutually unexamined married life. Ruth and Sam's dispute may have seemed frivolous, just the kind of thing all couples have to deal with. But it was a clear signal that neither of them had thought to redraw their "friendship map" once they married. Small resentments over unspoken expectations have a way of festering and growing larger.

The promise to forsake all others does not mean giving up your best friends or even relegating them to a minor role. It *does* mean taking the time—hopefully, before the wedding—to redraw your relationship map. Too many couples enter marriage thinking that their lives will basically go on as before, except now they'll have a soul mate to share it with. They view marriage as the icing on a cake that's already been baked.

I'm not saying that you'll have to start from scratch. Just be open to change. If "forsaking all others" means putting your partner first, what will that mean to your other relationships?

Sophia, a recently married friend of mine, asked my advice about how she could suggest a change in a long-standing tradition of her husband's family without starting a war. Her husband, George, came from a large, close Catholic family. He had seven siblings and many aunts and uncles and cousins. It was his family's tradition to gather at his parents' house after church every Sunday for a big dinner. When he and Sophia were courting, she gladly accompanied him. It solidified her special place in his life and gave her a chance to get to know his family. But once they were married, she began to resent the fact that Sundays were off-limits for anything else she wanted to do. During the week, George and Sophia both worked long hours. Saturday was usually taken up with errands. Sophia felt they needed Sunday as a day of rest. She carefully considered how she should approach George, realizing that this was an extremely touchy subject.

Sophia was a smart woman. She knew George would do just about anything to avoid a conflict with his mother, a formidable matriarch accustomed to having things her way. Sophia also knew that she didn't want to start married life by driving a wedge between their households. After all, one of the qualities she loved most about George was his devotion to his family. However, she felt entitled to have some say in the way they spent their free time.

It was an age-old question: How could Sophia be a loving wife, be supportive of her husband's desires, and also get her own needs met?

When faced with this dilemma, people often make the mistake of jumping into their demands for change with both feet, thereby creating an all-or-nothing standoff. Instead of starting off with a small request, they try to force their spouse into making a giant concession to prove that he or she really has *forsaken all others*. This approach harkens back to their childhood insecurities. In mature love, the goal is not to tear apart the old map of someone's life but to redraw that map while defining new byways. I suggested to Sophia that she begin with a small request of George, such as: "We're so busy these days, and I miss spending time with you alone. I would love it if we could pick one Sunday this month to just stay home and be together. Would it be helpful for me to call your mother and make sure it's not a Sunday when we would miss out on an important family event?"

Sophia's approach worked because she didn't plow into the discussion with a whine ("Why do we have to go to see your parents every Sunday?"), an insult ("I'm sick of your family"), or a challenge guaranteed to shame him ("Why can't you stand up to your mother?"). Rather, she expressed her feelings (the need for some time alone) with love (because she valued their time together). Furthermore, knowing George would have a difficult time communicating this request to his mother, she offered to make the call (respectfully, wife to mother-in-law) if it would make it easier on him. She made the offer in a manner that was not shaming to George. Ego fights and the need to exert power over your partner will cause you to lose every time.

It's a simple fact: Requests that are made in the spirit of love and respect are more likely to be acknowledged. When you avoid shame and blame, and let your partner know he or she is valued, conflicts fade from their heightened red-alert status and become more manageable. When your partner doesn't feel safe, energy is wasted in self-protection rather than expended in resolution.

Forsaking all others means that you are in this marriage together. You are partners, collaborators, allies in daily life. The following exercises will help unite you around your larger community.

Exercise 1: SET YOUR MARRIAGE TABLE

If you have open seating at your Marriage Table, I guarantee there will be bedlam. You need to make a seating plan you can both live with. This exercise will help you to do just that.

Exercise continued on next page

STEP 1: Sit down together and list all the people who are seated at your Marriage Table. These are the people (living and dead) who play a role in your lives, such as:

Parents
Siblings
Extended family
Ex-spouses/girlfriends/boyfriends
Children from previous marriages
Friends, both male and female
Clergy
Bosses
Colleagues
Neighbors
Beloved pets
Past influences

STEP 2: When you have created your joint list, take some time individually to place the names around your table. On separate sheets of paper, draw a big rectangular shape, representing your table. Place you and your partner at the center. Then, spreading out from each side, write the names from your list, as if you were making place cards for your table.

STEP 3: Share your results. How do your seating plans at the Marriage Table differ? Talk about your reasons for seating people where you did. Are there people who don't belong at your Marriage Table at all? Be honest about describing the roles others will play in your lives.

STEP 4: Take a third sheet of paper, and draw a new rectangular shape. This will be the table you set together. Take plenty of time making your final seating arrangements at the Marriage Table. You may want to work on it over the course of a week or two, until you're both satisfied. Keep in mind that your Marriage Table seating

Exercise continued on next page

plan isn't permanent. You can—and should—reset it as your lives evolve and change. (Births, deaths, new friends, job changes, etc.)

STEP 5: Establish a date once a year (not your anniversary, New Year's Day, or other significant dates) when you will review the place cards and reset your Marriage Table. Choose a time when you are both not emotionally charged or depleted from other events.

Exercise 2: **RULES OF ENGAGEMENT**

Each person brings to the marriage his or her own ideas about how to relate to others in the day-to-day course of life. That's only natural. You've lived separate lives up until this point. However, most of the couples I've seen never discussed their preferences in advance. Instead, they expected the square pegs of their differences to magically fit into the round holes of their marriage.
Separately take the following quiz. Be as honest as possible with your answers. Don't cheat and answer the way you think your partner wants you to. There are no right or wrong answers, just choices.

1. Work obligations always take precedence over relaxing with your partner.   Agree ❑ Disagree ❑

2. A platonic friendship with an ex is harmless.
                                                Agree ❑ Disagree ❑

3. It's important for couples to have close friends in common.
                                                Agree ❑ Disagree ❑

4. Holidays are times when the extended family should gather.
                                                Agree ❑ Disagree ❑

5. Birthday and anniversary celebrations are important.
                                                Agree ❑ Disagree ❑

Exercise continued on next page

6. Entertaining friends is fun.   Agree ❑ Disagree ❑

7. It's important to socialize with a spouse's work colleagues.

      Agree ❑ Disagree ❑

8. It's important to live close to your families.   Agree ❑ Disagree ❑

9. When family or close friends visit from out of town, they should expect to stay in your home.   Agree ❑ Disagree ❑

10. Your door is always open to family and close friends, even if they don't call in advance.   Agree ❑ Disagree ❑

11. If the phone rings, you should stop what you're doing and answer it, even if you are eating dinner, talking with your partner, watching a movie together, or cuddling.   Agree ❑ Disagree ❑

12. If a close friend needs money, you open your wallet, no questions asked.   Agree ❑ Disagree ❑

13. Casual flirting at parties is harmless.   Agree ❑ Disagree ❑

14. You should feel free to discuss problems in your marriage with a close friend or family member whom you trust.

      Agree ❑ Disagree ❑

15. You enjoy receiving spontaneous invitations to go out with friends.   Agree ❑ Disagree ❑

16. It's okay if your partner invites a friend to your home without asking you.   Agree ❑ Disagree ❑

17. It's okay for you or your partner to have friends of the opposite sex.   Agree ❑ Disagree ❑

Exercise continued on next page

18. You prefer vacationing with friends rather than as a couple.

Agree ❑ Disagree ❑

19. You can't bear to disappoint your mother. Agree ❑ Disagree ❑

20. If your parents lend you money to buy a home, they should have a say in your purchase.   Agree ❑ Disagree ❑

21. Your spouse should always come first, no matter what.

Agree ❑ Disagree ❑

After you have individually checked your responses, set aside time to review each other's answers. The goal is to open up a conversation about how each of you relates in the world. Try to avoid being judgmental; remember, there are no right or wrong answers here! You may even want to tape-record your conversation to create a record you can refer to later.

Begin with your points of agreement, and discuss what each of you was thinking when you gave the answer. This will strengthen your feelings of solidarity. Then note the areas where your answers differ. Let each person share the answer (without being interrupted), then discuss it together, using the techniques of mirroring, validation, and empathy. Don't expect to agree on every issue. The point is to acknowledge the areas where you have agreements and disagreements, and get into the habit of talking about how you will live your daily lives given this information. When couples are "awake" to their differences, they can more easily face conflict without wounding each other, and achieve resolution.

A NEW DEFINITION OF FIDELITY

Let's talk about fidelity, which is the essence of the vow to forsake all others. Sexual fidelity is essential to protecting the sacredness of a commitment. When a partner is unfaithful sexually, the injury is often fatal. That's because infidelity is about more than the act of sex. It breaks a primal bond. It brings harm to the protected union and violates the vows of safety, respect, and honor. Couples can recover when the virus of infidelity has stricken a relationship, but it requires the true and full commitment to deep remorse, regret, empathy, understanding, and of course a change in behavior.

What sets marriage apart from other close relationships is the total exposure. You stand naked before each other, accepting each other body and soul. No other relationship approaches this level of exposure or vulnerability. Affairs are illusions of intimacy. They don't provide a true context for mature love, which involves commitment to the real process of being known and knowing the other.

But what if a partner is sexually faithful and emotionally unavailable? Isn't that a form of betrayal as well? A couple I know was struggling with the tension between togetherness and alone time. She was upset because her husband was so distant in the evenings. She'd come home from work, eager to see him, and he'd say, "I need time alone."

HE SAID: I have a right to relax alone after a hard day's work.
SHE SAID: You don't have a right to ignore me.

Relationships don't survive automatically. They need to be nurtured with daily acts of affection. Everyone needs time alone, but if your idea of relaxation is to exit physically or emotionally from the marriage, you are being unfaithful to your emotional commitment.

Exercise 3: **CLOSING THE EXITS**

The vow to forsake all others means remaining available to your partner, staying in the present, and closing the exits that serve as escape valves from the marriage relationship. What are the typical exits? Ask yourself:

Exercise continued on next page

• Do you or your partner zone out in front of the TV every evening?

• Do you or your partner spend long hours in computer chat rooms when you are home together?

• Do you or your partner regularly get your emotional needs filled outside of the marriage?

• Do you or your partner spend long hours on the phone when you are home together?

• Is your idea of relaxation drinking alcohol that leaves you dozing in your chair by eight P.M. or zoned out emotionally?

• Do you avoid talking about your day with your partner?

• Are you like ships passing in the night, not stopping to hug or touch each other?

• Do you or your partner walk away when you're uncomfortable with a conversation you're having?

• Is giving or getting the silent treatment a regular part of your marriage?

Reflecting on these questions, ask yourself:

1. What are your exit strategies? What sets them off?

2. What are your partner's exit strategies? What sets them off?

3. What practical steps can you take to close your exits?

"Do, do not,
but there is no try."
—*Yoda, from* Star Wars

Five

For Better or Worse

To pledge commitment for better or worse is a lofty goal. What does "better" mean? What constitutes "worse"? Do we really mean:

> *"As long as it's mostly better, and as long as it works for me—and don't blame me if it gets worse—I promise never to go to sleep angry (so I'll toss and turn and keep you awake all night because I hate you); to forgive and forget (which is unlikely, given that my family members are the best grudge-holders in the universe); to fight fair (unless you really push my buttons, then the gloves are off); to give you the silent treatment for days and say 'Oh, nothing's wrong, I'm just feeling quiet,' when I want to punish you."*

Or . . .

> *"I promise to do everything in my power to keep things looking rosy, avoid any difficult conversations, go on vacations to places I hate (and silently fume but never say anything), to be long-suffering without complaining outright, but making sure you get the point that I'm miserable."*

This vow is about hope—the hope that, cross your fingers, everything will turn out for the best. The truth is, you cannot possibly envision the worst, nor should we try to destroy the optimistic spirit that is a blessing to a new union.

However, we should be realistic and acknowledge what we know about the tremendous toll that the stresses and strains of life can place on a marriage—either the accumulated strain caused by the burden of years of struggle, or the impact of a sudden, unmanageable tragedy. Research has shown that when the worst happens, marriages whose foundations are already shaky and uncertain often crumble under the pressure.

After September 11, 2001, our initial instinct as a nation and as families was to draw closer together. I knew many couples who voiced a renewed commitment to each other then. The impact of the attacks shook them out of inertia or anger and reminded them what they were about as couples. We all needed each other during that time, and we saw with renewed clarity the necessity of family and community bonds. But as the initial shock wore off, some marriages were unable to survive. Delayed trauma, deep psychic wounds, and feelings of despair can shift our world in ways we cannot anticipate or comprehend. This was especially true for those who were directly affected by the tragedies and/or were involved in the rescue operations at Ground Zero, the Pentagon, and the plane that went down in a Pennsylvania field. Years later, we have seen a sharp rise in divorce among firefighters and police whose lives were forever altered by the loss of colleagues, family members, and friends, and who spent long months immersed in the recovery efforts. Firefighters already have one of the highest divorce rates compared to other occupations, and catastrophe spikes the numbers. In the years after the Oklahoma City bombing, the divorce rate doubled in the local fire department and tripled in the police department; the early evidence is that September 11 may be no different.

We are also observing the toll that war takes on marriage. The divorce rate among military families has risen nearly 40 percent since the United States began operations in Afghanistan and Iraq. Deployment of spouses to far-off war zones brings extraordinary emotional, physical, spiritual, and financial stresses to families, throwing them into uncertainty and a survival crisis that no one could be well prepared to endure. Then, when soldiers return home, the initial joy is soon replaced by unexpected readjustment stresses. Servicemen and -women often carry traumatic physical and emotional wounds that change their lives and families forever. Statistics show that one in three returning military personnel is a victim of post-traumatic stress disorder (PTSD), which can haunt a person for the rest of his or her life. The figures are even higher among those with severe physical wounds, such as brain trauma, loss of limbs, or disfiguring burns.

Natural disasters, such as Hurricane Katrina, and personal disasters, such as the illness and death of a child, alter people's lives forever. I call this soul wounding. While some marriages collapse, others grow stronger. There are clues in your own marriage that can predict your ability to survive and even thrive when the worst happens.

LIVING IN THE LIGHT

We all have noticed that some people appear to have a special capacity for optimism and resilience, while others are easily driven to despair when the balance of their lives is upset. Resilient people survive and even thrive in the face of struggle. It stands to reason that resilient couples will be more likely to weather the large and small storms of life better than those couples who are fearful and unsteady.

Resilience is not just about recovering from hardship. It's not about what you do when the house caves in. It's about how you build the foundation in the first place. Resilient couples survive and even thrive in tough times because they did the work of creating a strong core. If your lie is that adoration, or romance, or sexual heat will keep you strong, your foundation will quickly turn to ashes in the face of adult challenges. If your lie is that all you need is each other, your reinforcements will be absent when you need them the most.

Exercise 1: YOUR RESILIENCE QUOTIENT

Can your marriage withstand the worst?

1. You know there are circumstances that your marriage could never survive. Yes ❑ No ❑

2. You feel that you deserve to be happy and are resentful when things go wrong. Yes ❑ No ❑

3. When you're confronted with a change, your first instinct is to worry about potential negative consequences. Yes ❑ No ❑

4. You'd rather say no and stay safe than say yes and risk disappointment. Yes ❑ No ❑

5. You are afraid that you or your partner will fall out of love. Yes ❑ No ❑

6. You feel most comfortable when you know you have control over your environment. Yes ❑ No ❑

7. You believe that sometimes the best way to handle a problem is to do nothing. Yes ❑ No ❑

8. You tend to dwell on past relationship failures and watch for signs that they are being repeated in your current relationship. Yes ❑ No ❑

9. You believe that you can't fully respond to another person without losing something of yourself. Yes ❑ No ❑

10. When you are disappointed, you blame the failure on your partner or on yourself. Yes ❑ No ❑

Exercise continued on next page

SCORE: If you checked four or more "yes" boxes, you are approaching your relationship from a place of fear. Fear is not the same as love. Fear clings; love expands. It's helpful to begin reflecting about where you learned to equate closeness with unending struggle. Chances are great that you will find the seeds of your insecurity in childhood.

THE TOXIC POWER OF OLD WOUNDS

From a very young age, Larry learned that he could not rely on his parents to nurture or protect him. Larry's mother was high-strung and ill equipped for parenthood. She was overwhelmed by the demands of caring for four children, and as the only boy, Larry bore the brunt of her impatience and short temper. She expected him to be well behaved, which to her meant controlling his emotions, his natural energy, and his curiosity. This was impossible for a little boy. When Larry's exuberance exceeded the allowable limit, which was fairly low for a growing and exploring child, his mother would often slap him or yell, "Get out of my sight and be quiet."

Larry's father was distant and rarely there. He worked long hours, and when he came home, the children were instructed not to "bother" their father. Larry adored his dad, but his father seemed disappointed in him. "He wanted me to be tough," Larry recalled to me, "but I was a little kid. I didn't know what it meant to be tough." Such early damaging and confusing messages require children to slice off parts of themselves to survive the wounding of parents who are often replaying their own childhood hurts. It is a cycle that will repeat itself down through the generations unless it is stopped by the healing truth.

One incident that occurred when Larry was five years old made a lasting impression on him. It was Sunday afternoon. Larry was in the yard, playing with his favorite toy, a mechanical fire engine, when two older boys from the neighborhood started bothering him. One of the boys grabbed the fire engine and said, "This is mine now." When Larry cried out and tried to grab the toy back, the other boy punched him in the stomach. He tried to fight, but he was knocked down. Larry was beside himself with fear and grief. He could not contain his sobs. He ran inside to the kitchen, where his parents were reading the newspaper and drinking coffee. As Larry choked out the story of what had happened, his father's face registered impatience and disgust. His mother looked horrified, but she made no move to comfort him. Finally, his father said, "You have to learn to defend yourself." Then he turned back to his newspaper, as Larry's mother slumped down in her chair, frozen by her fear of getting caught once again between her husband and her son. She felt that her husband was being too harsh, but her own inability to stand up to him, on her own behalf or her son's, made her go mute.

"I was five years old!" Larry cried indignantly when he recounted this story thirty-five years later. "How was I supposed to defend myself?"

From that moment on, Larry believed he had to take care of himself, because nobody else would. His parents made sure that he was fed and had a roof over his head, but otherwise he was on his own.

In college, Larry fell in love with Sonja, a warm, nurturing woman who gave him the kind of attention and affirmation he had never gotten from his mother, and the safety and respect he had never experienced from his father. Sonja's upbringing had been very different from Larry's. Her mother enjoyed being around her children, and Sonja and her three brothers were happy and secure. Sonja's father was a strong, capable man who always seemed to know what to do in a crisis. He was a loving father and a good provider, although he wasn't a hugger. Sonja idolized him, and she glowed when she won his approval.

Sonja was initially attracted to Larry because he was sensitive and physically affectionate. They connected on a deep level. She knew she could trust him to never betray her, and to stand by her through good times and bad.

But after Sonja and Larry had been married for a few years, Sonja became more and more impatient with him. The sensitivity she had once admired, she now saw as weakness. She wanted a man more like her father—strong, stoic, and resilient. In their frequent arguments, Sonja would taunt Larry to "stop being such a baby." Larry was always at a loss during these fights, as he tended to withdraw from face-to-face hostilities. He and Sonja drifted apart. Sonja began an affair with an older man who was the spitting image of her father in the way he dealt with his emotional life. Sonja left Larry and eventually married the older man.

The failure of his marriage drove Larry back into his five-year-old self, standing in the kitchen feeling that no one would support or comfort him. He told me he thought it had been a mistake to get married. "It only proved what I always knew," he said. "I have to take care of myself because nobody else will."

I encouraged Larry to see that the failure of his marriage might have been predictable—not because he had married the wrong person, or because no partner could be trusted, but because he had entered the union from a place of being wounded, and remained unaware of his wounds.

"You sought in marriage what was missing in your childhood," I said. "You chose a partner who would enable you to finally trust that another person would take care of you as your mother and father did not. You let down your guard, and it must have felt like a tremendous relief to lay that burden down. But when Sonja was unable to love you unconditionally, when she criticized you, it felt as if she had opened up an old wound. You withdrew, replaying the message 'Only I can take care of myself.' Your ideal left no room for her to disappoint you or for you to disappoint her and not personalize it."

The other side of the coin is that Sonja was also wounded. This could be seen in the way she attacked Larry as his wounds showed up more and more frequently. She needed a man to be "bigger" than she was, to be the problem solver and the leader. She was looking for Prince Charming to rescue her from the burdens of adult life.

To some degree, we all carry remnants of childhood wounds, and we seek healing in our intimate relationships. To be successful in marriage, individuals must know the difference between the wounded self and the true self. Your true self is the person you are beyond the fear. Your true self is the person you were born to be before all of the wounding of life, family, gender, ethnicity, and bias. The self that existed before society and culture, with all of its norms and rules, created schisms and barriers that barred access.

Ask yourself: "What would I do if I weren't afraid of losing, if I weren't afraid of rejection? Who am I, and who would I be if the wound weren't in the driver's seat of my life?"

HEALING THE SCARS OF RACISM

Racism and other forms of discrimination cause injury every day in America, and in the world, but it is in the marital union, in intimate partnerships, and within the family structure that it most often and profoundly rears it ugly head. Many couples are caught unaware of how the old wounds of not belonging, and the walls built up for self-protection, can take a toll on their happiness.

Don't minimize where you came from, what side of the tracks, the hue of your skin, the features of your face, or whether your family came over on the *Mayflower* or a slave ship. Don't ignore the impact if your ancestors were displaced when America was "officially" discovered, or if only part of your family survived the horrors of the Holocaust, leaving those who remained determined to keep a vow of silence, to protect themselves by never speaking of the atrocities of annihilation, demonic humiliation, and systematic extinction. If you are black and in America, don't rock yourself to sleep with lullabies of "Can't we all just get along?" Don't believe the fairy tales that tell of being rescued by a white knight, because those of us of African descent, who carry the dehumanizing horror of slavery, must find the beauty in a black knight that no one has ever written about, and one who never appeared in any of our childhood fairy tales.

I am inviting you to take a real look at your life, your history, and your hidden aches and pains, because if you don't they will continue to be uninvited guests at your marriage table, and they will be passed on to the next generation and the one after that.

Ronald and Mary were a happily married African American couple with three children. Ronald, a surgeon, was from a family of

physicians, three generations on his father's side and two generations on his mother's side. Mary, an architect with a prestigious
firm, was from a working-class family. Her mom was a clerk in the
town hall and her dad was a laborer in the Pittsburgh steel mills.
Life was good, until it came time for Mary to be made a partner in
the firm and she was passed over. She was very upset, and said she
would try again next year. But Ronald was fuming. He started calling Mary at work to ask how she was doing, wanting to show his
support, and then spending the remaining part of their conversation raging about racism, saying, "Mary, no matter what they are
saying to you, if you were white you would have made partner not
this year but three years ago. I can't stand this, and I think you
should quit. Give those white racists your two weeks' notice, and
tell them they can kiss where the sun doesn't shine." Mary was flab-
bergasted. She had never seen Ronald this angry. He was usually so
mild-mannered and trusting of the good intentions of people. He
often talked about his belief that, while life was not fair, it was important to keep one's cool.

Mary called my office, basically yelling, "Help, we're sinking!
I don't know what happened to my husband, but he is behaving totally
irrationally and I don't know what to do. I don't know how to get him
to calm down." While Mary agreed it was terribly unfair that she'd
been passed over for partner, she felt that something had snapped in
Ronald. He was a raging bull and she felt as if she didn't know him
anymore. "An alien has invaded my husband's body," she said.

Mary and Ronald came in, and we spent a few months doing
some very intense work. They exemplified the way that unresolved
issues from the past—not just your personal past, but the historical
past of your people—can still have an impact on you. Sometimes
the impact is positive and sometimes it is negative, but in order to
control it rather than it controlling you, the root issue must be exposed and understood.

Ronald had watched his parents struggle to achieve success in
their medical careers, and had heard many stories of previous generations of family physicians fighting the odds. He had never truly
assessed the cost of their struggles. He was afraid that if he did, it

would just make him angry, so he swallowed many of his feelings, much of his pain, and most of his healthy anger. He channeled it into becoming better than the best surgeon, and this is what his family had done, too. Mary, on the other hand, was much more aware of her feelings of racial injustice and unfairness, and while she thought she was coming to my office to get her husband back, they were both there to reclaim parts of themselves that they'd had to forgo just to survive. Each of them carried around hidden pain about how they had endured the aches and battering of racism. Mary's failure to get a deserved promotion had unleashed what had been lying just beneath the surface for both of them.

Ronald said during one of our sessions, "I learned how to put the wall up, to do my job better, to be nice even when I knew that people didn't want me to succeed. I tried to forgive patients who ignored my white coat and the red M.D. Surgery embroidered on my pocket, as they handed me their dirty breakfast trays to dispose of. I would just smile, reintroduce myself for the third or fourth time as the chief surgeon, and proceed with the medical business at hand. I never really asked myself what it cost me to be invisible. I never felt that anyone paid a price for this ignorance, including myself. It wasn't until Mary was passed over again for her promotion that I just totally and completely lost it. I was hounding her, calling her several times a day telling her to quit. She didn't know what had come over me, and I didn't know what had come over me."

I explained that when we "lose it," something wonderful is usually trying to happen. Some piece of truth is trying to float to the surface to help us back to shore. Ronald had erected a wall years ago, as he was taught to do by those in his family who had achieved professional success under great strain and strife. He was kind and approachable, and no one would have described him as walled in, but Mary acknowledged that she had felt the wall for years in his dealings with her and the children. She'd never understood it, and could not put her finger on it, but she knew that something kept him from fully giving himself to them.

The injustice and the unforgiving ache of racism had scarred Ronald, and he didn't even know it. It had imprisoned him and isolated him from his own truest feelings. He had erected a wall as a protection, not knowing that it kept out even those he most longed to be close to. During one session, Ronald wept as he recalled the stories his physician parents had shared of triumphing in all-white medical schools, with little support from professors or their fellow students, who often attempted to sabotage their efforts to excel. It wasn't until this session that Ronald realized he had lived with the same isolating pain of his parents all of his life, especially during medical school and his surgical residency. Mary's failure to make partner had shaken the wall of protection.

Walls of protection are not bad in and of themselves. They are erected when people experience danger—emotionally, relationally, physically, sexually, spiritually, or financially. Until the source of the danger is exposed and addressed, the wall will remain intact, often becoming more fortified as the years go on. The wall that Ronald had erected helped him survive the cruelties of racism, and the loneliness and isolation of his medical school years. But it became a barrier to intimacy in his marriage to Mary and with his children. When he demanded that she quit her job, it was less about what was best for Mary, and more about the generational racial wounds that were re-emerging for Ronald.

As Ronald and Mary realized that the pain of racism was an uninvited and destructive guest at their marriage table, they were able to have great compassion for themselves and for each other. They then made a plan for their own individual healing as well as the healing necessary in their marriage.

Mary said in one of their last sessions with me, "Dr. Smith, who would have ever thought that generational racism was threatening the well-being of our marriage? That seemed impossible. And, I want to be honest with you, when you first suggested it, I thought, 'Oh, no, we've picked the wrong therapist.' I now am scared to even think where we would be if we had tried to put a band-aid on our pain and on our marriage. We would never have made it. I was so sure that Ronald was just acting crazy, wanting me to quit my job. Now I know the pain of racism in his pot just got too hot, and boiled over—and this is how I got my husband back and the marriage that I had always longed for. It took this nightmare to wake us up to reality."

I want you to make the decision and choice that it will be you who stops the cycle of pain in your family, in your marriage, and most important, in your life. To do this, you must first really understand what the issues are and who it is that crashed your dinner party, and is sitting at your marriage table uninvited and unwelcome, stirring up a royal and painful mess.

THE ABANDONED CHILD

When Erin's mother died of a massive heart attack, Erin was inconsolable. And because they'd always had a rocky relationship, she was surprised by the breadth and depth of her grief. Erin's husband, Al, behaved like a rock. He stayed by Erin's side every minute, through all of the funeral arrangements, the funeral itself, and its aftermath. Al helped Erin pack up her mother's belongings and arranged to put her apartment up for sale. He took on extra parenting and household duties, trying to take the pressure off Erin.

But when weeks and then months passed, and Erin was still crying every day, disinterested in sex, and generally lackluster, Al's patience wore out. He gritted his teeth every time Erin morosely reminded him, "It's been thirty days [sixty days, ninety days] since Mom died." He resented her frequent trips to the cemetery. Why couldn't she just get over it already? Couldn't she see her family needed her? Couldn't she see how tired out he was from bearing the weight of his job and the family alone? When he tried to talk to her about it, he found himself in trouble.

AL: You've got to pull yourself together.
ERIN: How can you be so cold? She was my *mother*.
AL: Come on, get real, Erin! You were barely speaking to each other when she was *alive*!

ERIN: [*starting to cry*] Nobody understands. Nobody knows how I feel. Leave me alone. Just leave me alone.

When they came to my office, Erin looked deflated and depressed, and Al was seething but resigned. He started talking almost the moment they sat down. "Look, we're in our forties. It's not such a shock that our parents are going to die. My dad died three years ago, and I was sad, but I didn't fall apart. I can't take this big melodrama anymore. Some days I think we should have buried Erin with her mother. She's just not there for us anymore."

Erin flushed a deep red, and tears sprang to her eyes. "I know I didn't get along that well with my mom, but Al doesn't understand. One day she was there, and the next day she was just gone."

Few of us are prepared for the way the death of a parent brings to the surface so much hidden pain. Most people believe that the closer a child is to his or her parents, the greater the grief will be when they die, but sometimes just the opposite happens. Our most primal attachment is with our parent, especially our mother. When we are young, this attachment is necessary to survival itself. Often, when adults have troubled relationships with their parents, their problems are rooted in childhood hurts and the longing to be acknowledged and loved fully. Erin always felt that she had disappointed her mother, who was a highly critical woman. As long as her mother was alive, Erin held out hope that one day she would see her daughter with new eyes. In a real sense, Erin was grieving over her lost hope and missed opportunities.

Al thought by showing Erin she could count on him, he could fill that missing place in her heart and end her grieving. When she didn't respond to his love by "snapping out of it," he felt she was rejecting him.

Erin's mother's death presented them with an opportunity to explore the meaning of mature love in their marriage and on behalf of their own children. For Erin that would mean releasing her mother from the all-powerful position she held, even from the grave. It would also require Al to be interested in Erin's grief rather than to judge her, and to explore the triggers of his own impatience. In many ways he was mimicking Erin's mother's disapproval.

DO YOU LOVE YOUR BATTLEFIELD?

While in theory I understand and even agree, I cringe when I hear people say you have to pick your battles in a marriage. It reinforces the image that marriage is a battlefield, and this I reject. Marriage doesn't have to be and wasn't meant to be a bloody war, bringing endless suffering.

A man I know told me he was getting divorced. "I can't do anything right," he said. "Nothing pleases her. We've been to therapists and marriage counselors, and nothing has changed. I can't take the constant tension and screaming anymore. It hurts too much. This is too painful. I'd rather be left alone. I'm not God. I don't have the capacity to forgive her on a daily basis, but she does have the capacity to wound me daily."

It was a crucial understanding for him. There are occasions when someone chooses to remain abusive, and denial becomes a form of self-abuse and punishment. If you can't recognize the abuse and understand how your compliance helps it thrive, it is likely that you will stay stuck and feel victimized by this roller-coaster ride. You have to get off the ride. Sometimes that means leaving the relationship, sometimes not. But either way, you have to get off the ride.

This woman's capacity to blame and enflame was relentless. When she was hurt, she lashed out. She didn't know any other way. Her brutal style tells you something about her childhood. Somewhere she experienced brutality, overtly or covertly, and she initially developed a hardened manner in order to survive. It gave her a sense of being in control. She didn't even see how poisonous this behavior was in her adult relationships.

Why do people so often use negative tactics to try to enforce loving behavior? It seems counterintuitive. When our feelings are at their most intense, their most primal, they can drive us right back to the crib. The louder we cried as babies, the faster we were comforted, hopefully. As adults, when we are upset or feeling stressed, sometimes our screams of anger are cries to "hold me, comfort me, soothe me," but such cries do not belong on a battlefield, so our partners may respond by cutting us down.

Marriage is not meant to be one fight for power after another. I once heard someone say that you have to be a good soldier to endure marriage. Listen to those words—"soldier," "endure." They do not foster trust and safety. Rather, they evoke defensiveness and self-protection, which make passion and intimacy impossible.

As agonizing as these battles can be, I've often seen couples who have fashioned a comfort zone around their fights. It's almost as if they're saying, "I fight, therefore I am."

A couple I was counseling had been attending therapy sessions together their entire married life. I was their fourth therapist, and I immediately saw how comfortable they were in their pattern: She pounded away at him, and he sat there stoically, taking it all in with a blank face. The more she complained, the more vacant the look. Interestingly, she didn't seem to notice. She didn't want to open a dialogue, and neither did he. They weren't interested in trying to meet each other's needs. I wondered if they saw therapy as a game and me as the most recent pawn in their chess match. They could always tell each other and anyone who asked that they were in therapy, after all. It wasn't like they weren't trying to get along. I won't participate in this kind of sparring if that's the only point. Going to therapy sessions is not the same as being *in* therapy. I have often said to people that there is a difference between making visits to a therapist's office and being engaged in the real process of transformation.

In one of our initial sessions, I interrupted her litany of complaints to say, "You seem so unhappy. Why are you staying together?"

She was indignant. "I believe in honoring my vows," she said huffily. I could see that she had no desire to discontinue their therapy. She was energized by the fuel of her anger and the feeling of power and one-upmanship (or in this case, one-upwomanship) that she got from the sessions. She could boast that she was doing something to save her marriage, even though her "work" was an illusion. It was clear to me that she saw herself as better than her husband because she was the one who was most committed to therapy. This was just a grand form of acting out; she put him down to lift herself up. He played along, and neither of them had a clue about what was at stake.

"You don't need therapy for this," I said finally. "You can do this at home, and you can do it for free." And so I became the fourth therapist to put an unhappy end to their marital counseling sessions.

When couples hurt each other again and again, their marriages become a compound fracture: broken, not set right, rebroken. They're too fragile to heal. That's why, even when a couple comes to therapy *wanting* to heal, they need to understand that certain areas require a gentle touch, since they are easily rebroken.

The healing touch may require special promises, such as:

I will not bring up an old conflict without warning.
I will stick to the point of our discussion and not bolster my argument by recalling old hurts.
I will not expect you to read my mind.
I will not attack you when I really want a hug.
I will avoid using words like "never" and "always."
I will not discuss important issues at the beginning or end of the day, unless we have made a plan or appointment to do so.
When there is something important to talk about, I will make myself available to have the discussion.
I will talk directly and in short sentences so that neither of us gets overwhelmed.
If we need to stop the conversation because we are at an impasse, I will use wisdom and self-control to be protective of our relationship.
I will speak the truth respectfully, with the desire to maintain your dignity and my own.
I will not use derogatory or dismissive labels.
I will do the mirroring/validation/empathy exercise with you in a quiet setting, at a time when we both can listen and participate. When you regress, I will do my best to stay in my adult self, and I will make the same request of you.

And so on. The only way to win the war and leave behind the battleground is to choose a healing process that doesn't further compound the fracture. And it is important, particularly during conflicts, that at least one person remain an adult self. Two acting-out children make for a royal mess.

YOUR EMERGENCY PLAN

We all hope for the best, but hope without determination and effort often leads to feelings of frustration, disappointment, and hopelessness. You can write the vow "I promise to make you smile every day," but what about the days when there are no smiles to be found?

Life is going to throw you curves that you haven't anticipated—fire, flood, illness, job loss. Do you have a crisis plan? Do you have an emergency generator ready to provide power when the lights go off in your marriage? Do you have a relationship repair kit to help you recover from trauma?

There are different levels of repair. There are false repairs, which ultimately make the damage worse. There are patchwork repairs, which may hold things together in the short term but eventually wear away. And there are effective repairs that endure.

False Repairs

False repairs are illusions of repair that ultimately make the marriage worse. They're like fixing a leak by diverting the flood to another location. A man once told me he thought his fling with a coworker actually improved his flagging marriage. "My relationship with my wife got better when I was having an affair," he said. "I was more relaxed, happier, and didn't put so much pressure on her."

His definition of "better" was nothing more than an exit. It was certainly not a repair, since nothing was getting fixed. He didn't see how the betrayal of an affair eats away at the soul of a marriage.

Recently, I was browsing in a bookstore, and I came upon a book called *How to Save Your Marriage Alone*. It was an astonishing title, in my opinion. What exactly was being saved? Marriage is not a journey of aloneness. Its purpose is to create an environment where both individuals can be their true selves within the sacred bonds of the commitment.

Patchwork Repairs

When there has been a breakdown in the marriage—a fight, an attack, a broken promise, a disappointment—people often want to get over it soon and move on. They do a quick fix, hoping it will hold until they have time for a more permanent repair. But as with the fixes we do around our houses, other priorities get in the way of doing the permanent work.

Every time Sharon and Bruce had a heated argument, it ended with one or the other of them storming out of the room. They privately nursed their hurt feelings but never resolved the dispute. The day after one of these explosions, Sharon could count on Bruce arriving home with a bouquet of flowers. The first few times this happened, Sharon was touched by Bruce's gesture. She felt acknowledged. But over time, she began to see that the flowers were Bruce's way of avoiding further conflict. The problem that had initiated the fight never got addressed or resolved. Her resentment grew, and one day when Bruce arrived with flowers, she shoved them back at him.

Placating can be a patchwork repair if you don't know the difference between being relationship smart and just trying to keep the peace. What many people describe as making up is really collapse—throwing in the towel. Placating is a way to make someone less angry with you by going along with what he or she wants. Placating is someone saying, "I agreed to avoid a fight with her. I didn't feel like hearing her mouth." Or "I said yes to sex with him, even though he hasn't been nice to me, because I'm tired of him threatening to have an affair." There are many dangers to placating. It's exhausting and usually fear-driven. And the bottom line is it's lying. If you're lying because you're afraid you'll lose the relationship, you have a big problem. Something is broken, not just in the relationship, but inside *you*.

Patchwork fixes, such as makeup sex or the promise to never go to sleep angry, may get you through the night, but they won't resolve the problem. Over time, patchwork solutions can make the problem worse. Think about it. When you have a leak in your roof and you get it repaired right away, it is likely to cost less money and cause less damage to the interior of your home. If you wait and fill bucket after bucket while putting off repairs, the damage will be much more severe. When you avoid doing the work that is needed, there is always more damage.

Exercise 2: YOUR TOTAL REPAIR KIT

When a pipe breaks or a screw loosens or a chair leg wobbles, you get out your tools and fix it. If you don't have a tool kit, or crucial tools are missing, you cannot make the repair. And there are times that a fully stocked tool kit won't be enough, and it's important to know when you need to call in an expert to lend a hand in fixing what's broken.

Sit down together and make a list of what you need to have in your kit to get you through the hard times. Your kit should include qualities such as compassion, humor, and the willingness to listen and use the mirroring, validation, and empathy techniques. It should also include necessities, such as a good night's sleep, a healthy meal, exercise, meditation, music—whatever you know will help you quiet the storm until you can tend to it in a caring and strategic way. What I mean by strategic is that having a successful life doesn't happen magically. It happens with a plan, strategy, and the tools to execute your mission and desire.

Every person should have a repair kit on hand. Pipes break for unmarried people, too! Be sure to have your repair kit well stocked, so you aren't overly reliant on others, or desperate for rescue. Often desperation enters our lives though the back door of a rescue fantasy. Whether you are married or single, get rid of the rescue fantasy. It will steal your chance at creating a real life of love, connection, friendship, and joy.

RITUALS FOR BETTER OR WORSE

I have often observed one striking difference between marriages that thrive and marriages that fail (remember, your marriage can fail even if it doesn't end in separation or divorce, if it lacks joy, genuine passion, and mutual respect): the presence or absence of rituals. I'm not talking about religious services or even holiday celebrations, although these rituals can have great meaning. I'm talking about intentional rituals couples devise on their own to stay connected. Some of the most effective rituals are the smallest. For example, one couple sets aside fifteen minutes every evening to ask, "How was your day?" This is not a time to discuss the kids, finances, or the tasks that need doing, but to talk about themselves. They say to each other, "Tell me something great about your day." And "Tell me something that you wished had gone better or differently. Where did you shine? Where did you shrink?" It's the way they remind themselves that the other is important. The children know not to disturb their parents during this brief respite. Another couple celebrates the end of each week with a Friday poetry reading. They take turns choosing one poem that is a suitable meditation on the week. One couple I know writes a weekly love letter to each other. Another couple very close to me makes their love connection by taking walks, while other close friends take turns picking a movie that they want to share with their partner. Even if the partner isn't into the movie, they are into the special ritual of connection.

Rituals are a way of affirming connections, healing injuries, and creating joy. Sometimes the most meaningful rituals involve not what you do directly for each other but what you do together for others. Zoe and James met in a hospital emergency room. James had sprained an ankle playing touch football in a local park on a muddy fall afternoon; Zoe had taken a nasty spill from her bicycle coming down a leaf-strewn hill. It was a busy Sunday afternoon at the hospital, and it took hours for them to be seen by a physician. They didn't speak to each other until they were leaving and found their crutches colliding at the sliding glass doors. They took one look at the other and burst into laughter. They hobbled out to the parking lot together, and James playfully asked Zoe, "Would you like to have coffee with a jock—*not*." It was the start of a beautiful friendship that culminated in marriage fourteen months later. After their wedding and on the way to the reception, Zoe and James and the entire wedding party showed up at the emergency room where they had met. James carried Zoe over the emergency room threshold, everyone volunteered to give a pint of blood, wedding cake and sparkling cider were served, and a good time was had by all. Now, that was a terrific way to start a life together. Each year on their anniversary, Zoe and James each donate a pint of blood at the local Red Cross center.

Six

For Richer or Poorer

What could be simpler than to state that your love for another person is deeper than your love for your pocketbook? It seems like the clearest and most straightforward vow, the one least likely to be misinterpreted. Yet, as every marriage therapist knows, money is the trigger for more strife than any other topic, including sex.

Does the vow to commit for richer or poorer really mean:

"As long as I get what I need and look good in front of the neighbors, my family, and friends, everything will be fine. I'll expect you to be a good provider. Our children must go to the best schools and have the very best of everything, even if you have to work two jobs to provide it. And you can't really expect me to live in some cramped little space. You also have to understand that when I'm upset, I need to shop. And besides, I deserve it and I'm worth it."

Or . . .

"What's mine is yours, except the cash I'm socking away, just in case things go wrong, and the accounts I insist on keeping in my name only, because you never know what the future holds. Also,

you don't need to know exactly how much money I make. Please sign this prenuptial agreement on the dotted line—here, here, and here."

Or . . .

"If I want to take time off, or I have trouble holding down a job, don't forget that you promised you'd love me even if we were poor. Besides, you have a little something socked away, don't you, honey? Isn't there some money in your family? They seem to be doing well."

The major lie couples tell themselves about money is that it isn't an issue at all. Nothing spoils the romantic mood more than getting out the spreadsheets. It's not exactly pillow talk, and many people fear that if they discuss money during courtship, they'll be perceived as caring more about the bottom line than the love line. Besides, they figure if they're simpatico in other matters, surely they'll feel the same way about financial matters—more or less. The details can be ironed out after the honeymoon. (Never mind that for many couples, a wedding is the biggest financial transaction they've ever made.)

Does that sound like your attitude? If so, you're in for a big surprise. Chances are good that you and your spouse will have significantly different ideas about the role of money in your lives. How could it be otherwise? You were raised in entirely separate households and may have danced to completely different financial drummers. Whether you like it or not, these attitudes about money are deeply imprinted. Think about it.

What did money mean to your family when you were growing up? Did you always have enough? Were you comfortable, or were finances a constant struggle? Did you view yourselves as members of the "haves" or of the "have nots"? Were your parents lavish spenders or frugal savers? Was there a family budget or no budget at all? Did members of your family argue about money or never speak of it? Was there lying about money? Sneaking around? Was money a source of shame, envy, or feelings of entitlement? Was money equated with status? Was it used as a form of control and manipulation? Was money borrowed, lent, or donated? Was it spent on pleasure as well as necessities? Was money ever bartered for love or sex in your family? Did family members ever pretend to need financial help to appear dependent when they weren't?

The list is an endless one, stretching as far as your memories take you. You can see what a potentially explosive topic money is. It's extremely important that you come to terms with your separate financial legacies before your wedding. Or, if you are married and realize this is a hot spot for you and your partner, don't bury your head in the quicksand one more day. You will surely sink.

Exercise 1: YOUR INHERITED FINANCIAL ATTITUDE

Every individual enters adulthood with a financial inheritance composed of the experiences and attitudes of his or her family. Take some time to separately contemplate your own inheritance. When you've finished, share your responses with your partner, and discuss your common threads and innate differences.

1. Would you describe your family's financial situation when you were a child as poor, lower middle class, middle class, upper middle class, or well off? Describe the circumstances.

2. In your household, it was considered [gauche, rude, perfectly okay] to talk about money.

3. In your family, a generous person would be described as
_____. A stingy person would be described as
_____.

4. Your family's system of managing money involved:

_____

_____

5. You would do the following things regarding money differently than your family:

_____

_____

MONEY AND EQUALITY

Even in the most loving marriage, couples struggle with deeply held beliefs about the connection between money and power. In many marriages, there is an underlying struggle based on who is the "have" and who is the "have not" in the relationship. This can take various forms. For example, if one person earns a salary and the other is the family caretaker, there may be a perception that the person who brings home the money has more say in how it is spent, what part of the country to live in, whether to put the children in private or public school, if helping a family member is acceptable or not, or whether to buy a new car. Or if one person comes into the marriage with more capital, he or she may be perceived by both as having more power.

Mark and Eve, a couple I saw in my practice, were typical of this struggle for equality. They met each other in their forties, after both had been divorced for several years. Eve came from a wealthy Philadelphia family and owned a stunning town house in Philadelphia's historic Center City district. Her residence, built in the 1700s, had been exquisitely restored.

Mark made a good living as a tenured university professor, but he was somewhat hampered by debts from his previous marriage. When he met Eve, he was renting an apartment on the ground floor of an old house. His former wife had retained ownership of their suburban home in the divorce settlement.

During their two-year courtship, Mark and Eve spent most of their time at Eve's beautiful home, which bothered neither of them. Mark certainly had no desire to invite Eve over to his dingy bachelor rental. However, he was very aware that the Center City property belonged to Eve, and he was only a guest there. During their entire courtship, Eve never offered him a key to her town house, and he never asked for one, even though he sometimes had to wait outside for Eve on the street when she was running late to meet him there. Or in the morning, if Eve had to leave early, it was understood that Mark would get up and leave, too, even if his schedule didn't require it, because it was *her* house.

After they married, Mark moved into Eve's home, but even with his own set of keys, he didn't feel *at* home. Eve continued to refer to "my house" and "my furniture." When Mark gently suggested that they were a "we" now, she apologized. "I've been saying 'me' and 'mine' for so long now, it's become automatic," she explained. But reactions like that have a way of revealing deeper truths. When I saw Mark and Eve, they were two years into their marriage and locked in a full-fledged power struggle. For Mark, the problem was simple. He didn't think Eve viewed him as her equal.

"If I ask Eve straight out whether she thinks she's better than me because she has more money, she gets hurt and insulted," Mark said. "But if we have a fight and she gets angry enough, she'll point to the door and yell, 'Get out of *my* house.' I still feel as if I'm considered only a temporary visitor here."

Eve acknowledged that when she was angry, she sometimes played the money card. But she added, "Mark knows I don't really feel that I'm better than him. I didn't even graduate from college, and I become a total nervous wreck if we have to spend an evening with his university friends. The conversations, the political discussions, all of these intellectual arguments about art and music and the state of the world . . . I can't even keep up. It embarrasses me to think that Mark's colleagues and friends consider me some rich bimbo who Mark married."

"Eve, don't be silly. You've got a fine mind. I love you. You're no bimbo. I didn't know you felt that way," Mark said, amazed.

In that instant, the ground in the room shifted. "Intellectual accomplishment is a form of currency," I observed. "Understanding that may give you both a way to achieve the equality you've been seeking."

Watching this couple, I had the impression of a seesaw clanging up and down but never balancing. Each of them clung to the one thing they perceived as an elevating force—Eve, her wealth, and Mark, his intellectual acumen. But they had failed to meet on a middle ground where they could experience equality. Because they were aware and motivated, Mark and Eve had a good chance of finding that point of equality, beginning with the decision to purchase a condo that was truly "theirs."

You can't strip away your partner's dignity and hope for a real and lasting love connection. Nor can you offer up your own dignity as a sacrifice and wonder why the passion escaped through the front door. Maintaining your own and your partner's dignity is a fundamental requirement for a satisfying, committed relationship.

My patient Yolanda had a much sadder and more typical story to tell. A beautiful, exquisitely dressed woman in her early forties, Yolanda had been married for fifteen years to a wealthy and prominent businessman. Horace was twenty years older than Yolanda, and she was his third wife. They had two children together, and Horace had six children from his previous marriages.

Yolanda told me she had met Horace while working as a secretary in his company. Horace had just divorced his second wife, and he pursued Yolanda vigorously, with romantic dinners and expensive gifts. His passionate intensity was extremely flattering. Soon they were seriously involved.

"Then I became pregnant," Yolanda said. "I had been using birth control. I don't know how it happened. And Horace asked me to marry him. All my friends said, 'Oh, you're so lucky.' And I thought I was, too. But nothing in life is free. Materially, my children and I have everything we could ask for, and my children are indulged and happy—that's the trade-off. But for me, our whole relationship has always been a lie. I love my husband, but not in the passionate, intense way I would wish to love a husband and be loved by him. Horace makes me feel like an object, something he shows off to everyone, like a fancy new sports car. I know that every day of his life, he gets up thinking how lucky I am to be married to him. I want to be loved for me, not for just my beauty alone."

Yolanda convinced herself that she was making a worthy sacrifice by living in a loveless marriage so her children could be happy. "They get all of the benefits of this incredible lifestyle," she said. "They don't know how much pain I'm in. They don't know how I feel."

The only way Yolanda could feel good about living a lie was to think of it as a sacrifice she was making for her children. She didn't understand. The real lie was not that she wasn't in love with her husband; it was believing that she was a martyr for her children's happiness. Children possess finely tuned emotional radar. At twelve years old, Yolanda's daughter had already internalized the lessons she'd learned from observing her mother. She believed that to get what you want in life, you have to sell out: Your body and soul go to the highest bidder. No matter how wealthy and beautiful she may have seemed to others, Yolanda was deeply impoverished, and she was passing on that impoverishment to her children. She just didn't know it.

I found it revealing that when Yolanda talked about her son and daughter, she described them as "my" children. Although Horace was their natural father, Yolanda imagined them in the same role of supplicant that she was in. This, too, would leave an imprint on them.

Yolanda insisted she wasn't lying to herself about the trade-off she had made. She was even a little bit smug about it. But the deeper pain kept leaking through as she talked.

"Tell me," I said, "would you want your daughter to make a trade-off like yours?"

She was horrified. "God, no!" she said emphatically. "I pray she will have the love and happiness I've missed."

"Then you have to know that you are her primary model for what it means to be married," I told her. "She can't model something that doesn't exist."

My words struck a deep nerve. Yolanda had never considered this, and it was a disturbing moment of truth. "But what can I do?" she asked, stunned and helpless. I suggested she begin with honesty—first to herself, about her true feelings and the pain of living with a man who treated her like a piece of prime meat. Only after she'd gained some clarity into her own feelings should she consider beginning a dialogue with her husband. It may have been late in the game, but it was not *too* late. Several weeks later, she called to tell me that Horace had agreed to start couples therapy. This surprised her. She wondered if Horace cared more than she'd given him credit for. I admired Yolanda's courage. She didn't know it yet, but whatever the outcome, she would find that living in truth would open a previously locked door to satisfaction and even joy. And it was a priceless gift for her children.

PAYING YOUR WAY

Most young couples enter marriage with the expectation that their financial status will improve over the years. They see themselves as climbing a ladder that has only one direction: up. But life is not linear, financial security is not really secure, and private dreams and desires have a way of rising to the surface of one's consciousness when least expected.

Bill and Anne met when they were twenty, and they hit it off right away. They had grown up in the same neighborhood of hardworking blue-collar families, and they seemed to share the same values and goals—work hard, build a good life for your kids, and put family life above ambition. They often laughed as they recalled the well-worn mantra they had both heard as children: "We may not have much money, but we're rich in love."

When they were twenty-three, Bill and Anne were married in a modest, joyful ceremony. They scrimped and saved and bought a small fixer-upper house in their old neighborhood, close to their families. Bill had a good job as the assistant manager at a local hardware store, and Anne cleaned houses with her mother, who had a long-established housekeeping business. After a couple of years, Anne had a baby girl, Ashley. Between Bill and Anne's jobs, they made enough to pay their bills and still had some left over for recreation. Bill liked to go surf fishing, and Anne enjoyed going to yard sales with her mother and sister. They were happy, Ashley was thriving, and all was well. That is, until Bill's longtime employer decided to close his hardware store. Suddenly, Bill was out of work for the first time since he'd graduated from high school.

Anne wanted Bill to get a job at one of the big hardware stores in the local mall—Home Depot or Lowe's. The hourly wage was good, there were excellent benefits, and she was confident that

Bill would rise quickly to a managerial level. Her goal was to reestablish financial certainty as soon as possible. But Bill was intrigued by the possibility that he could do more. His friend Nestor had approached him about starting a business on the Internet auction site eBay, selling small household tools. Nestor knew someone who had developed a successful eBay business selling refurbished cell phones. The key, he said, was the ability to reach a global market.

"Think big," Nestor said.

"We have to think big," Bill repeated to Anne.

But Anne simply said, "No. Get a job."

Their arguments escalated.

BILL: I'm going to do this whether you like it or not. You'll just have to trust me.

ANNE: You're insane.

BILL: To have my own business is my dream.

ANNE: Since when? What happened to *our* dream?

BILL: What dream is that? The dream that you work like a slave until you retire old and bitter, and then die?

ANNE: Is that what you think of my father?

In my office, Anne said she felt betrayed by Bill's change of direction. She experienced it as a 180-degree turn that blindsided her. "He's not the man I married," she concluded.

Because Bill and Anne came from similar backgrounds, they assumed they shared the same view of the meaning of work in their lives. They had never talked about their dreams and expectations before they were married.

When Anne complained that Bill was not the man she had married, what she meant was that he was not the image of her father, the good provider. It was the quality she had most admired in her husband. But Bill was not her father.

Bill did not want to reprise the role of his own father, either. The strongest image he had from his childhood was of a tired, quiet man who was basically unhappy in his position as the sole provider for the family, and who had come home from work beat every night.

Bill and Anne's family imprints were visibly alike but essentially different.

Anne's Family Imprint
The men in Anne's family always had jobs with regular paychecks. They didn't take chances. They didn't borrow from their savings. They were steady, held on to their jobs, and were good providers.

Bill's Family Imprint
Bill's father always held a regular job, too, and was a good provider. But he was not a happy man. He didn't enjoy his work. He sacrificed his personal happiness for his family's security.

Bill and Anne were trapped by images from their young lives of role models that they had grown up to emulate. But their old family stories didn't allow them to create a new model for themselves. Anne believed that the only way to be secure was to have a steady job with a reliable paycheck. It was plain, however, that this belief was belied by the current reality of Bill's unemployment. I suggested to Anne that perhaps what she needed was assurance that Bill's dream had boundaries—that he wasn't jumping from a plane without a parachute.

I asked Anne to formulate a request of Bill, related to the new venture, that would address her concerns. She came up with the following:

ANNE: Bill, I request that we sit down with Nestor and work out the details of a business plan and then run it by our accountant. I also request that we agree to a set budget and time frame for the start-up.

I turned to Bill. "Is that a request you can fulfill?" I asked.

He was grinning. "Yes!" he said. "My wife has a good head on her shoulders, doesn't she?"

Bill's Internet business took off quickly, as many ground-floor businesses have. The rapidly changing environment of the Internet kept Bill and Nestor on their toes, and eventually, they hired a financial adviser and a marketing director. Bill and Anne learned that while it's important to know where the mold is set, it's just as important to know that it wasn't set in steel or stone. Often couples enter marriage invested in false roles. It's hard to create a marriage when the shadow of the superpowers called Male Provider and Dutiful Wife are looming over you.

KEEPING SECRETS

In a recent study, 26 percent of women and 24 percent of men agreed that money was the number one thing they were most likely to lie about and hide from a spouse. Lying about money becomes normal in some marriages. It's a way of taking back power that feels missing in the relationship, or of avoiding conflict. A friend whose husband feels she spends too much on the kids lied to him about who had paid for a clown she hired for her son's fifth birthday party. "We could afford the clown," she said. "But I knew it would lead to a fight. So I just told him my parents paid for the clown." She admitted to "fibbing" in this way two or three times a week, and she didn't see it as a problem. "What's the harm?" she asked. "I'm just trying to keep the peace. Big deal."

For many years, a man I know did not tell his wife about the annual bonus he received at work. He figured that since she didn't know about the bonus in the first place, she wouldn't miss it, and technically, he wasn't taking anything from the family. He, too, asked, "What's the harm?"

The harm is in the lie. I asked both of these people, "What are you afraid will happen if you don't lie?" Money was only the manifestation of a deeper sense of insecurity—a belief that it was dangerous to tell the truth. If there is one lie, there are other lies. The fabric of trust gets strained.

The man who lied about his bonus had a hard time understanding that. He believed that what his wife didn't know wouldn't hurt her. But with some prodding, he admitted that he assumed his wife lied to him about things, too. Since he knew she couldn't trust him, he figured he couldn't trust her.

The lack of trust is so familiar to many couples that they have come to accept it as the status quo. Yet fear of betrayal is a sign that the wounded, scared child is alive and well in the intimate relationship. Emotional maturity *insists* that we commit ourselves to finding safety in the truth.

Exercise 2: **MONEY SECRETS**

If you lie about money, even in seemingly insignificant ways, don't kid yourself. It *is* a big deal. Try to find the underlying fears that make it necessary to lie.

1. Have you ever hidden something you've purchased from your partner, to avoid an argument about money? If so, describe the situation. Write down the reason you felt it was better to lie.
2. Have you ever lied to your partner about the cost of something you purchased? If so, write down the reason.
3. Have you ever secretly put aside money? If so, why?
4. Have you ever lent money to a friend without telling your partner? If so, why did you keep it a secret?
5. Did you neglect to tell your partner about debts you brought into the marriage? If so, why?
6. Have you ever used money meant to pay a bill for something you wanted instead—and lied about it? Why?
7. What are you afraid will happen if you tell the truth?

THE PLEASURE PRINCIPLE

Peter and Marsha were both raised in hardworking, upper-middle-class families with similar earnings, investments, and property. Even so, their families had different ideas about how money was to be used. In Peter's family, money was rarely, if ever, spent on what he considered frivolous items. He was made to feel extremely guilty about spending money for his own pleasure. Marsha's family saved money for vacations, joined Christmas clubs, and enjoyed a weekly dinner out. A splurge for entertainment, such as a concert or movie, was considered money well spent.

Even though they both had good jobs, Peter and Marsha frequently fought about discretionary spending. A typical argument centered around planning a vacation.

MARSHA: I want to take a real vacation this year. Let's go far away, somewhere where we can really relax. I heard about a great beach condo in Hawaii for rent.

PETER: Marsha, you know we planned to paint the house during our vacation time this year.

MARSHA: We can hire someone to paint the house. I really need to get away.

PETER: I don't understand you. You wanted this nice house so much, now you just want to get away from it. I work too hard to throw money away on vacations.

MARSHA: I didn't know I was marrying Mr. Killjoy.

Is Peter right? Marsha? The truth is, neither of them is right. A conflict about money is not usually about being right or wrong. It's about being aware of your different money styles—preferably *before* marriage—and deciding how to resolve the inevitable disagreements that arise. It never fails to amaze me: I have counseled so many couples who never discussed the most basic concepts about money before they were married. You'd think it would come up long before the wedding bells started ringing. I'll chide couples in a playful manner: "You went out together, didn't you? Did you just take long walks accompanied by a chaperone? Didn't you ever go to a movie? Have a meal together in a restaurant? Go clothes shopping together? Rent an apartment?" Usually, they're shocked and somewhat embarrassed to realize how little they know about each other's true attitudes or hidden agendas regarding money.

Exercise 3: **MONEY VALUES**

Answer the following questions individually. Then compare your answers.

1. Once we're married, we should share our finances equally, regardless of who makes how much. This includes checking accounts, savings accounts, mutual funds, retirement plans, property, etc. Yes ❑ No ❑

2. Credit cards should be paid off in full every month. Yes ❑ No ❑

3. It's important to give money to charity. Yes ❑ No ❑

4. It's important for each partner to pull his or her own weight financially. Yes ❑ No ❑

5. It is acceptable for a woman to earn more money than her husband. Yes ❑ No ❑

6. You believe that "what's mine is yours." Yes ❑ No ❑

7. Dining out in restaurants is a waste of money. Yes ❑ No ❑

8. It's important to live a comfortable upper-middle-class lifestyle, with all of the luxuries/status that such a lifestyle implies (cars, house, furnishings, private schools, vacations, clothes, professional grooming care, etc.). Yes ❑ No ❑

9. A person should be free to choose his or her job, even if a spouse doesn't like it. Yes ❑ No ❑

10. It's harmless to keep small secrets from your spouse concerning your spending habits. Yes ❑ No ❑

Exercise continued on next page

11. Prenuptial agreements are necessary when one person has substantially more money or property than the other. Yes ☐ No ☐

12. Prenuptial agreements are a sign of mistrust.   Yes ☐ No ☐

13. Spouses should not be responsible for debts their partners incur before the marriage.   Yes ☐ No ☐

14. It's important to have a set budget and to stick to it. Yes ☐ No ☐

15. Families should support their elderly parents if they need financial help.   Yes ☐ No ☐

16. Parents should help their adult kids financially.   Yes ☐ No ☐

17. Occasional gambling or playing the lottery is a harmless expenditure.   Yes ☐ No ☐

18. It's important to look for bargains when shopping for household purchases, even if it means "spending" time to save money.
                                                    Yes ☐ No ☐

19. Children should have chores to earn an allowance and learn a sense of responsibility.   Yes ☐ No ☐

20. It's a sign of love to give your children the material things you didn't have as a child.   Yes ☐ No ☐

21. The stay-at-home parent should have as much value and input as the working parent.   Yes ☐ No ☐

Exercise 4: PRIORITIES CHECKLIST

How do your priorities about spending money match your partner's? The chart below lists typical expenses. To the right of

Exercise continued on next page

each item are numbers reflecting a scale of importance from 1 (less important) to 3 (more important) to 5 (most important). Individually mark the number that matches your personal priorities, then compare.

Name_____ Priorities Checklist					
Owning a house	1	2	3	4	5
Automobiles	1	2	3	4	5
Savings	1	2	3	4	5
Training/education	1	2	3	4	5
Having children	1	2	3	4	5
Health care	1	2	3	4	5
Clothing	1	2	3	4	5
Home improvement	1	2	3	4	5
Furniture	1	2	3	4	5
Supporting relatives	1	2	3	4	5
Travel	1	2	3	4	5
Entertainment	1	2	3	4	5
Cosmetic goods/procedures	1	2	3	4	5
Prior debts	1	2	3	4	5

Exercise continued on next page

Pets	1	2	3	4	5
Hobbies	1	2	3	4	5
Electronic equipment	1	2	3	4	5
Holidays/celebrations	1	2	3	4	5
Charity	1	2	3	4	5
Fitness	1	2	3	4	5
Other_____	1	2	3	4	5

Don't be deceived into believing that you don't need to do this if you have either few financial resources, or if you have a lot of money. No matter where you fall on the continuum of financial wealth, the issue of whether you see the glass as half empty or half full will impact your relationship and how you choose to spend or save money, and how you involve or exclude your partner. Don't fall into the trap of trying to sweep it under the rug. The pile of issues will just grow and begin to trip you in unexpected and costly ways.

Exercise 5: THE WINDFALL

Congratulations! You've just won $50,000 in the latest lottery drawing, or inherited it from the estate of a loved one. How will you decide to spend it? Individually, take a sheet of paper and do the following.
Write down how you would choose to spend a $50,000 windfall. Here are some suggestions:

Pay bills.
Get out of debt.
Buy a new sofa.

Exercise continued on next page

Put it in a savings or money market account.

Buy a car or a boat.

Put a down payment on a home.

Take a trip.

Make repairs on the house.

Start a college fund for the kids.

Help your elderly parents with a financial need.

Buy clothes and shoes for the family.

Donate some of it to charity.

Write down how you imagine your partner would choose to spend a $50,000 windfall.

Share your answers. Were you correct about your partner's answers? Were your ideas about how to use the windfall similar? Different? What do your differences reveal to you about your attitudes toward money? What did you learn that could be a problem or create an impasse between you regarding your views about money? What did you learn would be areas of relationship solidarity? What surprised you about yourself? What surprised you about your partner?

RELATIONSHIP RICHES: A SYSTEM OF CREDITS AND DEBITS

Being rich or poor isn't just about money and material goods. On a more fundamental level, it's about how you define worth and how you manage the give-and-take of daily life. How much do you invest in your marriage in time, activity, and goodwill? How much do you "spend"? Does one of you tend to invest more and the other spend more?

If you try to withdraw cash from the ATM and you haven't deposited money into your account, you'll receive a message: "Insufficient funds." The same is true in marriage. Often one person makes most of the deposits (of time, money, and love), while the other is always withdrawing those funds.

It's natural in a relationship to withdraw some of the goodies that attracted us in the first place—satisfying sex, good companionship, someone to be there for us when we get home after a long day, someone who is kind to our children—but there's often much more. We also want permission to take time off from work to care for an aging parent or growing children, the freedom to spend time with friends, and the ability to quit a hated job. These are all withdrawals from the relationship account. If one person is constantly withdrawing without putting enough back in, resentment builds. For example:

- You want sex, but you haven't spoken to your partner in days.
- You're eager to go golfing with friends, but for several weeks, you've ignored your partner's request that you go out for an intimate dinner together.
- You want to take classes at the community college three nights a week, but you don't make time for your family on the other evenings.
- You expect your spouse to accommodate your relatives over the holidays, but you don't pitch in to help.

Maybe you're investing more in the relationship account than you're withdrawing, but your investment often comes laced with complaints, anger, and martyrdom. That's comparable to writing a check, then stopping payment on it.

Understanding this issue and its origin in your life and relationships is the beginning of transforming a state of suffering into a state of reciprocity and receptivity. It is destructive to be on either end of the spectrum in your marriage, with your parents, siblings, coworkers, or friends. People who are always depositing can get into that dangerous role of being the long-suffering victim, a debilitating and deadly trap. It is just as dangerous to always be on the withdrawing end, which creates an atmosphere of use and abuse and the distorted sense of entitlement that permits this form of relationship destruction. A great marriage requires equity. It means trusting each other to show up as equal partners. The good news is that if you don't have that equity now, you can create it. Before you ever construct a family budget in dollars and cents, be sure your marital ATM is balanced.

Exercise 6: **YOUR MARITAL ATM**

Think about the past week. List five credits you put into your marital ATM. (For example, you cooked dinner three times and took your mother-in-law shopping without complaining.)

   1.

   2.

   3.

   4.

   5.

List five debits you took out of your marital ATM. (For example, you talked about your work problems for an hour, or you slept in while your partner fixed breakfast.)

   1.

   2.

   3.

   4.

   5.

Compare your lists. What have you learned about the equity that exists in your marriage?

"FEAR LESS, HOPE MORE, EAT LESS,
CHEW MORE, WHINE LESS, BREATHE
MORE, TALK LESS, SAY MORE, LOVE
MORE, AND ALL GOOD THINGS
WILL BE YOURS."
—*Swedish Proverb*

Seven

In Sickness and in Health

The promise to stay true in sickness and in health seems perfectly clear on the surface, but too often the subtext is:

"I thought your allergies were a temporary thing, not six months every year of sneezing and wheezing . . . and the dental bills are getting out of hand . . . and why didn't you tell me that cancer ran in your family? I didn't expect to be spending the prime of my life sitting in hospital waiting rooms. I feel terrible about your mother's ovarian cancer, but don't I deserve to be happy? Don't expect me to spend my golden years as your nursemaid. That's never going to happen."

Or . . .

"Your promise to love me in sickness and in health meant warts and all. I expect you to take care of me, even when I'm not willing to take care of myself. You know how I am. So big deal, I need a few drinks at the end of the day to relieve stress . . . and I'm one of those people who just can't quit smoking no matter what. And you'll just have to try and bear with me when I'm depressed or manic."

Or . . .

"I expect you to love me even if I let myself go. It's what's inside that really counts, isn't that right? You should also care about my health more than I do, but not nag and pester me into getting fit."

We tend to think that being healthy or sick just happens to us, not because of anything we do. Of course, we all hope for good health and naturally fear becoming ill or debilitated in any way. There is a deep wellspring of security implicit in the union provided by marriage, knowing that we can count on that special someone to be there for us if one of us falls ill. But it is also not uncommon to secretly fear that our spouses might stop loving us if we become a burden, or are no longer able to be full and active partners in the relationship. The balance in some unions depends on each person pulling his or her weight, and when that balance is upset, it's not uncommon for people to complain out loud or brood silently, "I didn't sign on for this!"

Few couples take the time (or wish to take the risk) to clearly define the potential implications of this vow before their marriage. And I'm not just talking about young couples radiant in the bloom of health. I've counseled older couples who married in their sixties and seventies and never shared their feelings with each other about caring for themselves or the other in case of illness. Now, there's a case of avoiding the elephant in the room! I've counseled military families who never talked about how they might deal with disabling war wounds, both physical and psychological. The fear is so enormous it leaves them mute. It feels almost as though a taboo is being broken, a superstition trod upon—as if to talk about it will make it happen.

Facing the vow to care for each other in sickness and in health is facing the truth. You are promising to strive together toward being the best you can be, engaging fully in the life of the body, mind, and spirit, pledging to take control of what you can, and working through what is beyond your control. It is a sacred pledge to stand together against the onslaught of time, aging, and disease, accepting the realities of biological life while holding on to your optimism about the future.

THE MEANING OF CARE

Foster and Jill symbolized the deal many couples make about health issues, which goes something like "I'll nag and you'll resist." When they came to my office, they were in real crisis. At well over three hundred pounds, Foster was red-faced and wheezing heavily as he sank onto the couch. He looked older than his relatively youthful thirty-five years. Jill, thin and nervous, sat straight-backed on the edge of her chair, her knees pressed tightly together.

Foster had gone to see his physician for his allergies, which had recently worsened. Alarmed by his poor lung capacity and weight, the doctor insisted that he be rushed by ambulance to the local hospital. The hospital kept him overnight for observation. Foster was then released but confined to bed at home for three days. Jill waited on Foster hand and foot, taking care of him in addition to looking after their two children, ages three and one. One evening, exhausted and resentful, she finally exploded.

"I'm lying in bed, sick, and she's screaming at me that she's tired of taking care of me, and saying she didn't sign up for this kind of misery," Foster recounted, his injured pride apparent. "I'm going, 'Well, what *did* you sign up for?' I felt she didn't even care."

Jill listened with a tight, angry expression, then said to me, "He thinks I don't care. That's so lame." She sighed. "This is an old argument. We've gone over this a thousand times. He's got it all covered. Nothing I say even matters. He doesn't listen to me."

"Look, Jill, I know I should lose a few pounds," Foster said. "I acknowledge that, okay? But with work and the kids, it's been hectic." Foster turned to me. "I've always been a big guy, but suddenly, Jill is on a mission to change me, and I resent it. The looks she gives me—if you could only see them. Her eyes . . . it's like she hates me."

"You've put on weight every year since we've been married, and we've been married for eleven years now," Jill countered. "You're at least seventy-five pounds heavier than on our wedding day. That's the difference now. That and the fact that you can hardly breathe—and you take all of these allergy and asthma medications, but you still smoke cigarettes."

Foster and Jill were both full of anger and built-up resentment. They could only continue to wound each other by going over the same ground again and again. Continuing this dispute led nowhere. I suggested we step back and try to find out what was really going on, using the exercise in mirroring, validation, and empathy to give them a chance to hear each other.

I asked Jill to swivel her chair around so that she was facing Foster on the couch. "Jill, tell Foster how you feel about this—not what you think he should do or what he's heard you say before—just tell him what you're feeling. Try to talk from your heart and your pain—not just your anger."

Jill thought for a moment and then said:

JILL: Foster, I love you, and I do care about you, but sometimes it feels like I'm the only one who cares. When you were hospitalized last week, I was terrified. I'm scared to death you'll just drop dead and won't be here with me while the kids are growing up. I want to help you, but I feel helpless in the face of your complete denial.

Foster immediately opened his mouth to protest, and I held up a hand. "Before you answer back, let's be sure you hear what Jill is saying. See if you can repeat it back to her, really getting the true essence of her words and feelings."

FOSTER: Okay, you said you were worried when I had to go into the hospital, and you're afraid I'm going to die and leave you in the lurch. Right?

Jill frowned. "That wasn't all I said."

"I think you gave a shorthand version," I observed. "Foster, if you're not sure what you missed, ask Jill to tell you again so you are fully able to accurately mirror it back to her."

As I stated earlier, there is often a need to resend the message, as most couples have grown used to not really listening to their partners when they speak. Rather, they are self-absorbed, talking or waiting to talk. So when they try to mirror their partner, they send back a distorted image of the communication. It is critical that we hear the true words and essence of our partner's feelings and that our defenses don't cheat us of the opportunity to heal the aches that have been plaguing our relationships.

"Foster," I said, "are you willing to ask Jill to please share with you again what she said that you missed? Remember, a mirror only reflects what is there, nothing more and nothing less."

"Okay," Foster said, shifting uncomfortably in his seat. "Jill, please tell me what I missed when I mirrored you."

Jill replied, "You jerk, you missed all that matters."

That was when the healing moment presented itself. "Jill," I said, "tell Foster what he missed that is 'all that matters.'"

"That I love him and care about him," she said, turning to me.

"Don't tell me," I said gently. "Look at Foster and tell him."

I knew that one of two things would happen. Either their defenses and ego protections were going to win, or vulnerability, honesty, love, and accountability would prevail and they would turn the corner on this blockage in the life of their marriage. I had a gut feeling that courage would be victorious with Jill and Foster. There was something clean about their fighting style. In spite of their frustration, their commitment and openness indicated they were ready to take the next step.

Jill turned toward Foster, her knees held even more tightly together than when she first sat down. She looked directly into his face, and before she could repeat her words, she burst into tears. I could see the shock and surprise on Foster's face, and then came his tears. Not a word had been spoken between them, but the cold protective wall was beginning to melt.

JILL: Foster, I love and care about you, and thinking of life without you terrifies me. I also feel like you don't care about me or the children because you neglect your health and your body, and I feel like you neglect us, too. I need you around, not just because I don't want to raise our children alone and because I would die without you, but because I need you and I want to grow old with you. I love you.

Before I asked Foster to mirror Jill's words, I asked her to tell us what her tears were about. She said that she had been so angry that she'd lost contact with how much she did love Foster. It felt good, she said, to realize how deep her love and desire for her husband went. This is an important point, because couples can become so entrenched in the power struggle and in the blame and martyr game that they lose touch with the foundation of their goodness and the goodness of their partner.

Foster mirrored Jill beautifully. Something had shifted between them. Each was interested in what the other was sharing, and even when the truth was painful, I taught them to say "Ouch" and be mindful that they were treading on the sacred ground of pain and transformation.

"Foster, do Jill's feelings make sense to you?" I asked. "Would you say they're valid?"

"I have to say yes." Foster was weeping, and Jill had his full attention.

"Can you share with Jill how you imagine she feels?"

Foster was able to empathize genuinely with the fear and frustration that Jill had been feeling. He could also empathize with her great love for him, because he loved her so.

I then explained that Jill's promise to care for Foster "in sickness and health" did not mean that she was responsible for picking up all the pieces, or caring more than Foster himself cared. "Caring without boundaries is the definition of a victim," I said.

I asked Jill to write down the promises she could make that would demonstrate care within boundaries. She came up with this list:

Jill's promise:

I promise not to care more about your health than you do.
I promise not to nag you or beg you to take care of yourself.
I promise to support you in the specific requests you make, such as not bringing sweets into the house, or arranging

appointments with a doctor, or joining you for daily walks.

I promise to be honest with you in a respectful way when I am feeling upset about your self-neglect.

I promise to hold you accountable to what you've promised to the kids and me.

I promise to remind you that I love and care about you, and to treat you like an adult, not a child.

"Jill cannot force you to lose weight or stop smoking," I told Foster. "And you wouldn't want her to. But your decisions affect her. The lie you're telling yourself is that it's your body and your business what you do, and Jill should back off unless you want her to take care of you. In that case, you think she should be your loving, nonjudgmental nurse. But Jill has a right to ask you to show up as a grown-up and be a full partner in your marriage."

I worked with Foster and Jill on understanding what childhood issue this impasse represented for both of them. Foster became aware that he'd never had any help as a child addressing his needs, but he'd received plenty of feedback about how he was falling short. Because of this wound, he had been unable to hear Jill through the clamor of critical voices from his past. When Jill was growing up, she had been the one who worked her buns off to keep her family healthy. She'd been groomed to take responsibility for things that were not her responsibility and then resented the heck out of people when they didn't change. Jill and Foster were re-creating their childhood hurts in their marriage. Fortunately, they were committed to fixing what was broken, placing responsibility where it belonged, and taking action toward a new contract that could work for both of them. Also, they were willing to be held accountable by themselves, by each other, and by me. They were showing up and actively doing the work to grow up so they could reap the benefits of a satisfying love connection and true partnership.

The vow to be committed in sickness and health means that you will strive for health—not just physically but mentally and emotionally as well. That means both of you. One man told me that his wife wanted more for him than he wanted for himself; she was more invested in his health than he was. You can take a horse to water, but you can't make him drink. This is the lesson for all enablers. You can't make them drink, and in trying to make them drink, you end up killing your own life spirit.

SELF-CARE COMES FIRST

Many women pour themselves so completely into the care of their families that they leave nothing for themselves. They place themselves last on the list and never get around to self-care. They wear their physical exhaustion and emotional strain as a badge of honor. The more they do for their loved ones, the more acceptable it becomes to let themselves go. Women believe it's okay to become the sacrificial lamb on the altar of their personal family values. This is a lie that we, as women, have allowed ourselves to buy in to. The challenge for women is to reinvent a way to be loving wives and mothers that does not require them to put themselves last.

If you don't take care of yourself, you cannot care for others. That's a fact. It's like the message you hear on an airplane when the flight attendant instructs, "In the event of an emergency, if you're traveling with a child or with someone who needs assistance, put your own mask on first." The point is clear: If you are going to be of any use, you have to be able to breathe. You have to be alive.

A big part of self-care is allowing yourself to be human. Media and society frequently communicate the message that women need to portray themselves as "together," capable of performing any task thrown their way. But when women look at the reality of how often they feel overwhelmed in their own lives, they may actually feel they aren't good enough or worthy enough. Women often compare themselves to other women who appear as though they are "doing it all"— and when they size themselves up in comparison, they feel inadequate and become overwhelmed. But you can't show up in your own life and expect to make a lasting impact if you are on the run.

When you become overwhelmed with striving for and failing to achieve perfection, the fear will cripple you. The internal barometer that gauges, guides, and directs your life as an empowered woman—that lets you know you are enough and okay—is broken and needs to be fixed.

Marlene was depressed by the weight she'd put on since she had a baby. She felt that she'd let herself down and let her husband down. "I was always one of those girls who had all of the cutest guys at school chasing after me," she said wistfully. "I married a very handsome man. I used to say he was the pick of the litter. We were a stunning couple on our wedding day. But now I've let myself go. I weigh over two hundred and twenty pounds, and I hate myself. I didn't realize how bad it was until I was in the local supermarket last week and ran into one of my old boyfriends. He didn't even recognize me. I told him who I was, and I could see by the look on his face that he was appalled and disgusted. I knew he was thinking, *What happened to* her? I was humiliated. I, too, wondered, *What happened to her? Is she lost and gone for good?"*

Marlene was overwhelmed by her feelings of failure. The climb back to self-esteem seemed too far. She felt ashamed that she was no longer the woman her husband had married.

"It was a lie you told at the altar," I said. "You stood there in your beautiful dress, beside your handsome fiancé, and promised that you would always be perfect, no matter what. You'd be his super-heroine. Now you're ashamed because you couldn't meet your own impossible standards." Until Marlene understood the lie (that she needed to be perfect to be loved) and replaced it with the truth (that she was worthy of love just as she was), she could not begin to take care of herself in a meaningful way. As she embraced this truth, she found herself with new energy and motivation to take care of herself. Being overweight was one of the chains that began to fall away.

SEXUAL HEALTH

Does the following scene sound familiar? Mary and Gayle are best friends. As women do, they are confiding in each other, talking about Gayle's new romance. Mary asks, "Is the sex good?" Gayle beams. "Oh, yes, it's great," she gushes. "He's so turned on by me. He says I'm sexy. He loves my body. He loves making love to me."

Notice anything? I'll give you a clue: *He . . . he . . . he . . . he.* Not one word about how Gayle feels or whether *she* is turned on. Her entire focus is on his desire for her.

I believe the real reason women struggle with having orgasms is that they're so busy setting the stage, so busy pleasing, out of fear and cultural pressure, that they place no focus on being pleased. Many women think, *If he's excited about me and I've pleased him, I'm a good lover.* But maybe you're just a good actress. Essential to being a good lover is the ability to receive pleasure as well as give it.

Women are socialized to please, not just in the kitchen but in the bedroom. Sex is an especially tricky area, because the total intimacy, the complete exposure and nakedness of lovemaking, can trigger many of our most basic fears and a sense of vulnerability.

For instance, many women falsely tell themselves that:

I have to have a great body to be sexually desirable.
If my partner has an affair, it means I'm not satisfying his needs.
His sexual satisfaction matters more than mine.
If the sex is good, our relationship can withstand anything.
If my partner has trouble performing, it's because I'm not a good enough lover.
If my partner wants sex, I should force myself, even if I'm not in the mood.
If my partner wants sex and I do it even though I don't want to, he will cherish and honor me.

Every one of these beliefs is a lie, but the lies gain power because they are never confronted and debunked, and they are reinforced daily in the media and society at large.

Of course, there's a whole other side to the sexual dance. What does the male in the relationship want sexually? What are his misperceptions and insecurities? What are his expectations? What are his fears?

Male sexual dysfunction can be laid at the door of many

causes—overindulgence in food, alcohol, or drugs; inadequate foreplay; disinterest; medications that interfere with libido; a woman's inability or unwillingness to arouse him; fear of not performing up to expectation; age; gender stereotypes of what is acceptable sexual behavior; and a lack of understanding that the sexual relationship can be satisfying to both partners.

Don't go into marriage assuming you know each other's attitudes about sex, or what your differing sexual needs are if you haven't talked about them. Don't even assume that just because you have a sexual relationship before marriage, you necessarily know all you need to know. Before marriage, couples exhibit their "presentational selves," and that's true even for couples living together. A woman once called my office, hysterical, three days after her wedding. Her new husband, with whom she had lived for two years before marrying, announced on their wedding night that it was "extremely important" to him that they engage in a particular sex act she found abhorrent. He had never mentioned it the entire time they'd been together. "He said he didn't think it was appropriate to bring it up until we were married," she cried. "But he claims that the Bible says there is no abomination that a man and his wife can commit with each other, so it's okay. Now he expects it, and I don't think I can do it."

Know your sexual needs and preferences before marriage, and that means understanding the imprints made in childhood.

Exercise 1: YOUR SEXUAL IMPRINTS

Your primary role models for sexuality were your parents. That may seem strange, since most people have trouble thinking of their parents as sexual beings. But the imprint was made. Consider the following questions:

1. Were your parents physically loving toward each other?
2. Did your parents have affectionate nicknames for each other, or otherwise demonstrate what you now recognize as playful flirting?

Exercise continued on next page

3. Were discussions of sex taboo?

4. Did your mother or father have a serious conversation with you about your sexuality when you reached puberty?

5. Were there different attitudes about expressing sexuality for the boys and girls in your family?

6. What were your parents' attitudes about gays and lesbians?

7. Did your parents believe that sex before marriage was sinful? Was this true for the boys in your family as well as the girls?

8. Did you feel comfortable confiding in your mother or father if you had questions about sex?

9. Did your parents ever argue about sex or about sexual behavior, such as flirting at parties?

10. Was there an aura of shame or openness concerning sex?

11. Was sex used to cover up deeper problems?

Sharing your answers with your partner is a positive, relatively nonthreatening way to open a dialogue about your own sexual life and what your beliefs, hopes, expectations, and needs are.

ADDICTION: THE BIGGEST LIE

I have tremendous compassion for people who are in relationships with addicts. Addiction is powerful and compelling. As I discussed in the introduction to this book, I've been there myself. I spent too much time with a man who was addicted, and as much as I loved him and cared about him, I was helpless against the power of his addiction.

Here's the secret about addicts: They are often incredibly seductive. They can be the most charismatic people in the room—the most fun to be with, and seemingly the most spiritually alive and sensitive of souls. An addict has the ability to sweep you off your feet better than almost anyone. They're excellent sales persons. What I now know that I didn't understand during my relationship is that an addict is more attached to the addiction than to anything or anyone else. It was an illusion that my partner was spiritually alive or sensitive. It was exactly the opposite. He was spiritually dead and fully cut off from his ability to care about me or anyone else in his life. Just remember, my willingness to be entangled with such a man grew out of my illusion that I could get him to change for me. I thought if he cared enough to give up his addiction for me, it meant I had value. I had not yet learned how to find value in myself. I was lost and in search of my spirit. Whew! I'm so glad I don't live at that address any longer, and that I left no forwarding information for my low self-worth to find me.

Nora met Donald at a bar where she was having drinks with a group of friends. He dazzled them with one hilarious story after another. She hadn't laughed so much in years, and all of her friends hoped that they'd be the one singled out by this charming, witty man. Nora was very attracted to him, and when he called for a date the day after they met, she was thrilled. All her friends were terribly jealous of her. Nora and Donald dated for a few months, going out constantly to restaurants and bars, and they always had fun. Nora had such a good time that she ignored the fact that Donald was usually drunk by the end of the evening. Soon Nora was head over heels in love.

When Donald invited her to take a vacation with him to the Virgin Islands, she was thrilled. He rented a little cottage on the beach, and Nora looked forward to an intimate week of fun and romance—sunbathing, sailing, romantic walks on the beach, and long, dreamy nights. But her fantasy was shattered almost as soon as their plane departed.

An hour into the flight, Donald had already consumed four airline bottles of Scotch. Much to Nora's embarrassment, Donald turned into that "other man"—the person he became when he was drinking. While he seemed charming, he became overly familiar with the flight attendant, who clearly understood that he was high and had too much to drink; she had to ask him to quiet down twice as he was watching movies and laughing and talking too loudly. Things were a little better once they had landed and arrived at the cottage, which was everything Nora had imagined: serene and elegant, with a breathtaking view of the brilliant blue sea. They dropped their bags and headed for the beach, where they spent a beautiful afternoon, tropical cocktail after tropical cocktail magically appearing, served by the attentive staff of the resort lodge. Donald was extremely relaxed, dozing off and loudly snoring between quick bouts of consciousness and sips of the potent rum drinks. As the sun lowered in the tropical sky, they began to walk back to the cottage. Donald was intoxicated, and he clearly had no awareness of the state he was in. He was talking to Nora as if he weren't drunk. He made inappropriate comments and kept referring to the sex he was interested in having. The last thing on Nora's mind was having sex with someone so inebriated. His overtures weren't romantic; they were offensive and disrespectful.

As they approached the cottage, Nora noticed the figure of a man relaxing in a lounge chair on the deck. As they got closer, she recognized him and her heart thudded. It was Donald's brother, Ken. What was he doing here?

When Donald spotted his brother, he yelped with delight and ran to greet him with a big hug. "You made it!" he cried. Nora watched, stunned, as the brothers discussed plans for the evening. When Ken went off to buy a bottle of tequila, Nora finally said, "You didn't mention that Ken was coming."

"Oh, didn't I?" Donald asked distractedly. "Well, he wasn't sure he could make it. Why ruin the surprise? It's good this place has a pullout couch."

Nora spent the first night of their vacation alone in the beautifully appointed little bedroom, while Donald and Ken played loud music in the living room, put away a bottle of tequila, and then stumbled off to find a beach party where they could continue their "unwinding." Nora cried herself to sleep and was awakened by a drunk Donald standing over her, saying how much he wanted to make love with her. She was stunned that Donald had the nerve to approach her for sex in this state. She thought, *This is the furthest thing from lovemaking I could imagine.* But they had sex, which she knew beforehand would be a mistake. Donald was so drunk that he wasn't there. Nora felt like an object, just something else for Donald to use to make himself feel better. The next morning, after

Donald and Ken went off to drink some more and go fishing, she packed her bags, and left on the next flight out.

"I wish I could say I learned my lesson," Nora told me years later. "But he showed up at my door a week later, so abject and apologetic that I took him back. After that, every time he got drunk and did something crazy, he always convinced me that he was truly sorry, and we'd have a wonderful night together. Then it would start all over again."

Nora was trying to achieve the impossible task of creating a partnership with someone who was not available—someone who was not even in the room, let alone in the relationship. Eventually, Donald even stopped apologizing—insisting that Nora was the only person who complained about his drinking. He was trying to flip the script—make it *her* problem. Nora finally stopped trying to accept what was fully unacceptable. She realized he had chosen his habit over her, and there was nothing left to save.

Nora's experience with Donald is typical of the perverse and isolating dance of addict and enabler. Even more often, I've seen examples in my practice of couples who self-medicate with alcohol or drugs as a way of exiting their relationship. These are the people who equate relaxation and stress relief with substances. It's important that you know up front that you're partnering with someone who will basically check out with a few drinks after a hard day of work, or amid the stress of caring for a chronically sick child, or if there are financial pressures. You can't have a partnership if one or both of you passes out chemically high by eight every evening or stays up late at night having an affair with the substance of choice.

Eventually, alcohol, marijuana, cocaine, pills, and pornography have a way of catching up with you. They have a way of destroying all of your meaningful relationships, too. Anyone who grew up in a household dominated by any form of substance abuse knows that this is true. Unfortunately, as adults, we often mirror the destructive behaviors we witnessed growing up. That is why the children of alcoholics are often alcoholics themselves, or they partner with alcoholics. This cycle of addiction and abuse can be broken, but not while living the lie of denial. It can be broken only if the addiction is exposed and treated and all of those impacted are helped as well.

Exercise 2: **ARE YOU A SELF-MEDICATOR?**

You don't have to get drunk to be an alcohol abuser, if you're using alcohol as a way to exit your relationship or handle the ordinary stresses of life. Ask yourself:

• Do you grab a drink when you need to calm down?
• Is pouring a drink your relaxation ritual at the end of the day?
• Does your spouse, significant other, or your child complain to you or talk behind your back about your drinking or drug problem?
• Do you have trouble remembering the last time you didn't have one or two alcoholic drinks or glasses of wine with dinner?
• Do you drink "too much" on weekends or when you're on vacation?
• Do you feel entitled to a drink or your substance of choice at the end of the day?
• Have alcohol, drugs, or pornography ever caused the end of a relationship?
• Does it make you nervous to know you're going to a social event where alcohol will not be served?
• Did your mother or father use alcohol as a way to relax?
• Have you been told that you change or act differently after you've had a drink? Has more than one person told you this?
• Do you feel that you deserve to drink because you work hard?

What promises can you make to each other about being present in your marriage, rather than choosing an exit by self-medicating? What promises are you willing to make to keep your partner safe and honor your marital vows? An addiction is a self-absorbed and self-indulged illness. Do you expect your partner to stick it out with you when you have chosen your substance abuse over him or her? These are tough questions that must be asked in order to make wise choices.

Exercise 3: HEALTH ATTITUDES

Before you make the promise "in sickness and health," figure out what each of you means by that. Answer the following questions individually, then use your answers to have a truthful conversation.

1. I believe every person is responsible for his/her own health.
Yes ❑ No ❑

2. There's nothing wrong with relaxing with a drink or smoking marijuana at the end of the day. Yes ❑ No ❑

3. If my partner smokes, that's his/her problem. Yes ❑ No ❑

4. It is inevitable that people will put on weight as they get older.
Yes ❑ No ❑

5. If he/she gains weight, I have a right to be displeased.
Yes ❑ No ❑

6. I have a right to a certain amount of sex, regardless of my behavior. Yes ❑ No ❑

7. I expect my partner to get regular health checkups.
Yes ❑ No ❑

8. It is my partner's responsibility to schedule his/her medical appointments. Yes ❑ No ❑

9. "In sickness and health" doesn't include mental illness.
Yes ❑ No ❑

10. "In sickness and health" doesn't mean living with an addict.
Yes ❑ No ❑

Exercise continued on next page

11. I have a right to know my partner's personal and family health
histories.   Yes ☐ No ☐

12. If I get sick, I expect my partner to take care of me.
                                              Yes ☐ No ☐

13. When I am mean or disrespectful to my partner, I still expect
him/her to be sexual with me.   Yes ☐ No ☐

14. If my partner gets sick, I still expect him/her to fulfill me sexually.
                                              Yes ☐ No ☐

15. I expect my partner to be sexual with me when I'm intoxicated.
                                              Yes ☐ No ☐

16. There is nothing wrong with using pornography to meet my
sexual needs.   Yes ☐ No ☐

"Live as if you were to die
tomorrow. Learn as if you were
to live forever."
—*Mahatma Gandhi*

Eight

Till Death Do Us Part

When we say "until death do us part," do we really mean:

*"As long as I'm not sick to death of you . . . as long as you can
continue to turn me on . . . as long as you're able to keep your
figure . . . as long as you keep your hair . . . as long as you
continue to make me feel all mushy inside . . . as long as someone
better doesn't come along."*

Or . . .

*"I'll stay with you until death, because I don't believe in divorce.
But I'll live in misery and, believe me, so will you. Not only that,
I'll let everyone know it. I'll be a martyr to my vows and wear
my suffering like a badge of honor."*

The promise to commit oneself to another person until death is
serious business—unless, of course, it isn't. There is no more
powerful example of a lie told at the altar than this vow. The irrefutable evidence is the divorce rate, which has hovered around
50 percent for decades. One of every two marriages does not
sustain itself until physical death. Many other couples die emotionally, spiritually, sexually, and sensually within the marriage,

but they feel obliged to "honor" their vows to stay until the bitter end. These unions of quiet—and sometimes not so quiet—despair are broken long before the physical death of one of the partners. They are divorced, just not on paper, not by law, and not according to their religious practice. I imagine, though, if you were to check the record of honesty and integrity held in the Court of the Sacred by the Keeper of All Records, you would find that the true "divorce" rate far exceeds 50 percent.

I believe there should be two mandatory questions asked of those who are planning to get married: "What will make your marriage not only last but be satisfying and mutually rewarding?" And "How do you plan to keep yourself from getting sucked into the vacuum of divorce and despair?"

Vowing to stay together for life is an empty promise, unless the vows leading up to it have real meaning for you. Just parking yourself on the couch to watch TV for fifty years does not make a solid marriage. It can make for a long marriage, but long marriages don't necessarily equal satisfying and happy marriages. When people say they've been married for a long time, I am always careful not to assume that I know what the longevity of the marriage means. It could mean that I am looking at a solid and mature couple who have found a way to truly love, honor, and cherish each other. It could mean that I am privileged to witness a couple who chose to show up and grow up. It could also mean that I am looking at a couple who deserve to be awarded the title "Martyrs of the Century."

I know a woman who tried in every way not to lie at the altar about staying married until death. "I was raised with the idea that you go to college and then you find a husband and get married," said Coralee, a thirty-eight-year-old art dealer. "While I was at college, I fell in love with a very nice man. But at the same time, I was beginning to tap into what I really wanted in life, and at graduation I knew I wasn't ready for marriage. Unfortunately, the universe *was* ready—my boyfriend, his family, my family, our friends. Everyone except me. I kept telling people I wasn't ready to get married, and they'd tell me, 'I hear what you're saying, but it's just cold feet.' I was being swept along, and I wasn't sure how to stop it.

"My fiancé and I went to our pastor for premarital counseling. I told the pastor straight out, 'I have no problem going through with this, but you have to take out the line "until death do us part," because I'm not going to stand before God and make a promise I'm not sure I can keep.'"

If Coralee thought her words would bring the wedding to a halt, she was wrong. "Everyone, including my fiancé and our pastor, thought that was cute—just Coralee being Coralee, honest and bold," she said. "So I took the path of least resistance, and we got married. He was a nice man, but we had absolutely nothing in common. Our life goals went in opposite directions. After a few years, I realized it wasn't fair to him for me to keep up the lie, because he wanted children and I didn't." She realized she had done this because it met everyone's needs except her own.

On their fifth wedding anniversary, when Coralee's husband raised a toast "to next year," she sadly told him there wasn't going to be a next year. This was how she honored him and herself.

Another woman told me that right before she walked down the aisle, her father turned to her and said, "Just remember, you're a Catholic. Being a Catholic, you can drink, you can smoke, you can dance, you can gamble. You're not allowed to do those things in every religion. But you *can't* get divorced. Do you understand?" She did. And she also understood when, after her divorce at age thirty-nine, her father said disgustedly, "And to think you used to be the *good* one." Still, it was a sobering realization to know her father would have preferred that she stay in a loveless marriage until death.

Even great marriages have bad days, and sometimes bad years. Periods of conflict, boredom, stress, and hardship can and do afflict every couple. That's not necessarily a bad thing; it's something that happens in the course of living a life together. The question is: What do you make of it? What does it mean to you?

THE FANTASY RETURNS

From the vantage point of the altar, as you stand there with optimism and joy in your hearts, your future stretches out before you as an exhilarating glide down a rose-petaled path. Who wouldn't want such a destiny? Till death? Gladly! This is the moment when the lie is so seductive, so romantic, so powerful, it sweeps you away along with it.

Seven or ten or twenty years down the road, the bloom is off the rose petals, and your reaction might be "You expect me to do this until *death*?"

When the film *The Bridges of Madison County* was released, I remember watching it and thinking that it would keep me in business forever. It created such a longing in women. It seduced them out of the everyday routine of their lives, filling their hearts with the potential for true and spontaneous love. A mysterious, handsome, sexy, sensitive stranger would suddenly appear out of nowhere, and they would fall madly in love with him. He would say the words their husband no longer said, rekindle the passion that had died or never been sparked, and express the adoration that seemed a distant memory. On the screen, it looked good to me, too. I knew better, but those movies *do* call to a young, primitive, and immature part in all of us. This is not to say that deep passion isn't possible, just that it is created genuinely only in the context of a committed relationship. We have almost no images of this type of love and passion, so we are stuck with our unfulfilled longings from movies and love songs that make us crave more of the illusion and less of what we could really have if we cultivated it.

In the story, a rugged but intelligent stranger—a wandering photographer taking pictures of covered bridges—shows up on the doorstep of a world-weary country wife. He arouses an intense passion in her that has lain dormant for many years. She stirs awake and comes alive again. It's a wonderful fantasy, but it isn't real. Let's face it: Strong, sensitive Clint Eastwood look-alikes aren't wandering the countryside, knocking on remote farmhouse doors in search of their soul mates. What was real in this woman's life was her marriage to a husband who took her for granted, and the love of her children. And even though a true love existed between the couple, there was a dead zone in their marriage. The affair with the photographer was a jolting revelation, but it was also an illusion. It wasn't a solution.

The fantasy does happen. It returns to catch us unaware when we are tired, or vulnerable, or lonely. My friend's cousin was swept off her feet by a man she met while vacationing on an exotic island paradise. She had been through a particularly grueling year, and she desperately needed a vacation trip to lift the heaviness in her life. Although she knew little about the man she met on her fantasy island, she fell hard. She believed he was The One, the great love she had searched for all of her life. He was everything she had ever dreamed of—tall, handsome, kind, charming, and a successful surgeon to boot. They were married within months. When he said he planned to open a clinic for children scarred by war, her heart filled with love for him. He was so good and so giving. She told him she would be honored to invest her savings in his new practice. She believed in him and wanted to support his dreams.

After they had been married for almost a year, her handsome surgeon husband kissed her goodbye one morning and left for work. He never returned. Later, she discovered that he wasn't who he'd said he was. He wasn't a surgeon. He was a con man and former convict with a rap sheet a mile long, whose modus operandi was wooing lonely women and marrying them, then taking their life savings. He left my friend's cousin completely heartbroken, humiliated, and financially shattered.

My friend told me how vulnerable her cousin was: The con man had zeroed in on her vulnerability like a laser beam. Manipulators, power-mongers, people who have no remorse and no conscience, can sniff out a good victim. They reel out their predatory lines. A victim will take the bait, while a nonvictim will either ignore it or bite back, saying, "I'm not the one for your games." I hoped that this woman would learn from her experience by growing wiser and stronger, but it was a struggle for her. When my friend challenged her, saying, "You're still in love with him, aren't you?" she replied "yes" immediately. Then she qualified her answer with "I mean, I'm still in love with the man I married."

Ah, I thought. *That's it!* The man she had married didn't exist. He never existed. That was a myth. She was in love with a fantasy, and it was terribly hard to give up the dream of what she'd thought he was and what she'd imagined their life would be.

It took over two years before my friend's cousin could say the name of her betrayer without choking up. It wasn't until she finally talked with three other women, former "wives" of this con man, that she was able to move on. Even then she couldn't get over the magnitude of the lie—that a man could stand with her at the altar, never intending to keep his promise to love her until death. She was the sad witness to the reality that a marriage based on a lie cannot thrive.

I recently had this same discussion with one of my own cousins who was grieving over the loss of an illusion—not the loss of a real person. The man she was involved with was so shameless in his behavior that there was nobody real to love. My cousin said to me, "Well, we did have some good times together," and I replied, "Yes, slaves were sometimes treated nicely by their masters, too, but that didn't mean they weren't slaves. The nature of slavery meant that the foundation of the relationship was always destructive. Don't be deceived by a few moments of so-called good times. If you put them on a scale against the bad times, they wouldn't even budge it."

EVEN IF IT KILLS YOU?

Every nine seconds a woman in the United States is beaten by her partner or spouse. By some estimates, one in three women will experience at least one physical assault by an intimate domestic partner in her lifetime.

If you are in a relationship where there is physical abuse, you have to ask yourself this question: *When I promised "till death," did I really mean until it killed me?* And if you are in a relationship where there is emotional and verbal abuse, you have to ask yourself: *When I promised "till death," did I really mean until it killed my spirit and my soul?*

Love doesn't batter. Love doesn't demean. Love doesn't send you to the emergency room. Love doesn't huddle with you in a corner, crying your eyes out. Love doesn't scare the wits out of you. Love doesn't make you wish you were dead. If you believe it does, then you're living a lie.

Love is gentle, it is kind, it doesn't keep score of wrongdoings. Love forgives, it repents and shows remorse, it changes its way when it has gone down the wrong path. Love affirms and makes room for differences; it makes safety and honor its backbone, and a sense of aliveness its gift.

I am speaking mainly of women here because, although domestic violence against men does occur, it is only a tiny fraction of what women experience. Many people can't understand why a woman stays in an abusive marriage or relationship. The real question is why a woman enters a relationship with an abusive man in the first place. The ground has to be fertile in order for abuse to take root in your life. An abusive man will not be able to stick around, much less make it to the altar, with a woman who is strong and secure in who she is and what she wants—a woman who truly loves and cares for herself. It takes a frightened woman with damaged self-esteem to believe the lies an abuser uses to justify his behavior. He tells her that his explosive anger is deep passion; that he wouldn't get so mad at her if he didn't care so much about her; that he has never met a woman who gets to him as deeply as she does; that he loves her so much it makes him crazy, wild with jealousy: "I hit you because I love you so much."

A man can come into your life and behave horribly, and if you value yourself, you'll think, *That guy is bad news*. But when you let him sit at your table, sleep in your bed, move into your house, and share your meals, it's a sign that your self-worth has been badly compromised. Maybe you grew up being told that you didn't count for much, that you weren't pretty enough, that no one would ever want you or love you, and you don't think you deserve more.

A woman whose live-in boyfriend almost killed her explained to me why she had taken him back. "I love him too much to let him go," she said. "And I believe he loves me, too, although I know he may not always show it the right way." She also confessed, "I love him more than I love myself."

I told her the truth. "You don't love him," I said. "It only feels like love to you because you don't know who you are without him. That's how abusers work their way inside. They convince you that you need them, and they call it love. If you continue to support that fantasy and live that lie, it will eventually cost you your life."

If you are married to an abuser and you stay in the marriage because you are afraid to leave, or because religious beliefs forbid you to break your vows, or for the children (and how could staying in an abusive relationship benefit the soul, spirit, or psyche of a child?), you need to know two things: First, your life matters, and it belongs to you. Second, your partner broke his vows long ago. What you have is not a marriage. It's a prison sentence, and the only question is whether it's life without any possibility of parole, or the death penalty. Is your partner your jailer or your executioner?

A woman who summoned the courage to leave her emotionally abusive husband once cried out to me, "Why did it have to get so ugly and hurt me so badly?" She meant the breakup, but it was much more than that.

"It hurt so much because, long ago, when the ache first started, it was a small throbbing," I said. "You accepted it. You said, 'I can live with this.' Then the ache became deeper, and you accepted that, too. You said, 'I can live with even this.' And when the abuse became almost too much to bear, you said, 'That which does not kill me makes me stronger.' Can you see what happened? It was a gradual process. You took action only when it had become unbearable. It's like discovering that you have cancer. If you ignore the symptoms, it will grow to kill you."

One of the goals of emotional, relational, and spiritual maturity is the ability to self-protect as well as to show honor to others. Honor must be earned. You give honor when it is due, and you withhold it when it is not. Otherwise you become party to a growing lie. Have you ever been to a funeral for someone you knew well who wasn't kind to many people, and as you listened to the glowing eulogies, you wondered who in the world they were talking about? To be healthy, you have to be able to call abuse what it is—abuse.

A close woman friend of mine has an amazing young daughter. One day, while the girl's grandparents were watching her, her grandfather made an extremely cruel remark to her. Later, with tears in her eyes, the girl told her mother what her grandfather had said that deeply hurt her feelings. My friend was brilliant in her response. She explained to her daughter that her grandfather had been mean, that her grandmother should have stopped him from hurting her, and that it would never happen again. My friend said all of this in the presence of her parents, to make sure they knew that her father's overt cruelty and her mother's silent collusion were unacceptable and would not be tolerated.

The next day the little girl went to school and was sad. Because she was an outgoing and talkative child, her teacher asked her, "Stacey, why are you so quiet?" Stacey recounted the incident with her grandfather, and her teacher said, "Oh, well, your grandfather is old. Old people are grouchy and cranky sometimes." Stacey said, "No, my mommy told me that what he said was *mean*, and that it was not okay for him to ever speak to me like that again." The teacher realized that Stacey's mother had given her an invaluable lesson. She had taught her to identify abusive behavior, no matter what its source, and that she had the right to protect herself from anyone who attempted to harm her, including her grandparents.

I was deeply struck by this story, because most women did not receive clear messages when they were young about mental, verbal, or physical abuse, and were therefore unable to recognize it and protect themselves. This girl's mother understood that her daughter needed a true frame of reference, and she gave her a priceless gift.

TRANSFORMING FAILURE

Dr. Harville Hendrix has said that relationships can be incubators for growth and healing, if we allow them to be. Even if your marriage ends in divorce, you can move away from the blame and hurt and use what you learned in a positive way. If you leave your relationship, don't leave without the lessons you've learned. Whether you leave or stay, learn the lesson. It's never about him or her. Maybe he's a jerk, but you have to own your collusion in allowing him to become a bigger jerk over a span of twenty years together. Maybe she's negative and judgmental, but you need to own your willingness to allow her negativity to infuse your life. If you don't own it, you'll repeat it.

Maybe your marriage won't end in divorce, but it will live in despair. I want you to know there is a third choice.

An unhappy couple came to see me. They said, "Divorce is not an option."

I told them, "Continuing as you are is not an option, either." I am pro-commitment but not for needless suffering. "You need to find ways to invite something different from each other that will allow you to thrive." They found this a radical idea. Their goal in coming to me had been to find a way to endure a life that was unsatisfying, and they were stunned when I suggested they find a way to have a great marriage.

A Japanese proverb says, "When death finds you, hope that it finds you alive." If you are going through the motions, spiritually and emotionally dead, does it matter that you stayed until the bitter end? Do you want your tombstone to read, "I endured until death"?

When you make a vow to be with another person for as long as you both shall live, you are vowing to be alive in your marriage. To do otherwise is to squander God's most precious gifts—life and time.

Nine

Eyes Wide Open

When I work with married couples, I often find myself asking, "Did you discuss this before marriage?" We could be talking about money, sex, children, jobs, spiritual practices and beliefs, just about anything. Chances are, the problem they're stuck on was never even considered before they were married. I'll say, "Since neither of you is a mind reader, and there is no crystal ball, how did you know your partner's attitude?" They'll usually shrug and look embarrassed, but they don't know why they failed to do their homework. I think the easiest explanation is that many couples fear if they discuss difficult, potentially controversial issues before marriage, the whole thing might blow up. When people are falling in love and courting, they prefer to highlight the similarities between them rather than any potential differences. So they keep silent and hope for the best.

Most of us have learned to think of hope as the opposite of fear, the winged dove that will transport us into the future. But hope without action is not true hope, and hope removed from action creates frustration and despair.

I prefer the philosopher George Santayana's more solid concept: "Those who cannot remember the past are condemned to repeat it." Learning the lessons from yesterday comes from continuing to ask the questions about what has worked in your life and what has not.

I invite you to look at what it means to start marriage with your eyes wide open, using the following 276 questions as a pathway to the conversation of your life. By that I mean an ongoing conversation, not a one-night stand. And please don't say that you don't have time right now to ask these questions. You will pay the toll to marriage either now or later, but there is no getting across the marital bridge without paying the toll.

There's a saying in the black church that everyone wants to get to heaven, but no one wants to die. Everyone wants the inheritance, but no one wants to pay the tax. It's that same longing that many people bring to marriage. Everyone wants a great marriage, but few of us have been willing to do what it takes to create one. As I was ending my destructive relationship, my partner told me, "Robin, I really want this to work." My response was "And I want world peace, but ask me what work I've done lately to truly bring about world peace." My point is simple: What you put in is what you get out. If you want to make chicken stew, you don't put beef in the pot and then wonder why there's no chicken. What you want to get out of your marriage you must put in, and you must have a partner who shares your goals, objectives, and key values.

There is no crystal ball, but you don't need one anyway. What you need is the courage to ask yourself and your partner the hard questions and be willing to accept the truthful answers that come from the process. Finding out what is important for your sense of well-being and for that of your mate is key in building a strong and sturdy marital foundation. If you're afraid that exploring certain issues will rock the boat and capsize your relationship, then you don't have the relationship to weather the storms of married life.

Do not approach your conversation from a place of confession or judgment, but from a place of honesty, with an openness to learning. The purpose is not to see if your partner matches your criteria. It's not a checklist. I urge you to look beyond the superficial and consider those qualities required to withstand the long haul.

Curiosity is a wonderful gift to a marriage. It allows a couple to transform an attitude of blame into inquisitiveness about the world of the other. The posture of curiosity in marriage creates a platform from which new conversations are birthed, and it unlocks the treasures to be discovered in another's uniqueness.

If you are already married, you may be surprised to learn something new about yourself and your spouse. If you don't currently have a partner, this exercise is still important. Getting to know yourself is a prerequisite to having a successful relationship. I call this the No Surprises Toolbox. As you reduce the element of surprise about important issues, about everyday issues, and about all the things you take for granted, you are stabilizing your foundation. As you stop playing the guessing game and the "let's pretend" game and commit to truth, you increase your chances of creating a happy and mutually satisfying marriage.

276 QUESTIONS TO ASK BEFORE YOU MARRY

Work

Let's acknowledge that we live in an extremely status-oriented society, with emphasis placed on marrying a person with the "right" professional identity. How often have you heard people brag (or maybe you've bragged yourself) about a partner, saying, "He's a doctor" or "She's a model," as if status alone were enough to guarantee a good relationship. Unfortunately, you don't hear people bragging, "He's a kindergarten teacher" or "She's an administrative assistant at a not-for-profit organization in the Bronx." This is part of the problem. When we focus on status, we destroy any chance to live an authentic life with a partner who shares our values.

These are the questions you really want answered:

1. Are you working in your chosen profession?
2. How many hours a week do you work?

3. What does your job entail? (For example, do you often travel for business, work at home, perform dangerous tasks?)

4. What is your dream job?

5. Have you ever been called a workaholic?

6. What is your retirement plan? What do you plan to do when you stop working?

7. Have you ever been fired?

8. Have you ever quit a job suddenly? Have you changed jobs a lot?

9. Do you consider your work a career or just a job?

10. Has your work ever been a factor in the breakup of a relationship?

Home

Details about where and how you actually live may seem secondary to weightier matters. That's especially true if you're young. But questions about your nest are primal. Home is the place that shields you from the world, and you need to know whether your home will be a sanctuary or the eye of a storm. Begin by asking your partner these questions:

11. If you could live anywhere in the world, where would it be?

12. Do you prefer urban, suburban, or rural settings?

13. Is it important to have your own private home, or do you prefer apartment or condo living, with a management company responsible for the maintenance? Are you a do-it-yourselfer, or would you rather hire professionals? Do you prefer to clean your own home or hire a housekeeper?

14. Do you think of your home as a cocoon, or is your door always open? What do you need to feel energized and inspired in your home?

15. Is quiet important in your home, or do you prefer having music or some background noise most of the time? Is it important to have a TV in the bedroom? Living room? Kitchen? Do you like to sleep with the TV or radio on?

16. How important is it for you to have a space in your home that is yours alone?

17. Have differences about home style ever been a factor in the breakup of a relationship?

Money

As we discussed in Chapter Six, money is a loaded topic. Many couples stop talking at the point of "how much," assuming the rest will take care of itself. But questions about money will infuse themselves into every area of your life and show up on a daily basis. These are a few of the questions you should ask:

18. If you had unlimited resources, how would you live?

19. How important is it for you to make a lot of money?

20. What is your annual income?

21. Do you pay alimony or child support?

22. Do you believe in prenuptial agreements? Under what circumstances?

23. Do you believe in establishing a family budget?

24. Should individuals within a marriage have separate bank accounts in addition to joint accounts? Do you feel that bills should be divided based on a percentage of each person's salary?

25. Who should handle the finances in your family?

26. Do you have significant debts?

27. Do you gamble?

28. Did you have a paying job when you were in high school? Before high school?

29. Have you ever been called cheap or stingy?

30. Do you believe that a certain amount of money should be set aside for pleasure, even if you're on a tight budget?

31. Have you ever used money as a way of controlling a relationship? Has anyone ever tried to control you with money?

32. Has money ever been a factor for you in the breakup of a relationship?

Relationship History

When relationships don't work out, people often assume that it's because they chose the wrong person. Some people even enter marriage with a soothing unspoken exit, thinking, *If this marriage doesn't work, I can get divorced and just try again.* But you need to understand that all relationship exits are cheap, in that they cheat you out of the true lesson you need to learn in order to create rewarding and lasting love. You'll remember in the introduction to this book, I described my own childhood wound as the fear of being insignificant and not existing. I carried this wound into my adult relationships and found ways to avoid it, but didn't face it until the man I was with actually did erase me and replace me. Facing that painful reality allowed me to wake up from a coma-like sleep. Mature adults do not view the erase/replace mode as a viable option for creating lasting love. Thinking that you can erase someone from your life and replace him or her with someone else, without addressing the true issues, will only lead to continued failure. It's important that you know whether you or your partner has this tendency.

33. Have you ever felt deeply insecure in a relationship? Were you able to name your fear?

34. When was the first time you felt that you were in love with another person? What happened in that relationship, and how have you come to terms with it?

35. What is the longest relationship you have ever had prior to this one? Why did it end, and what lesson did you learn?

36. Have you ever been married? If so, are you divorced or widowed? How do you think you handled the loss?

37. If you have a current partner, do they know of behaviors that you exhibited in your previous relationship that you're not proud of?

38. Do you believe that past relationships should be left in the past and not talked about in your current relationship?

39. Do you tend to judge current partners on past relationships?

40. Have you ever sought marriage counseling? What did the experience teach you?

41. Do you have children from previous marriages or nonmarital relationships? What is your relationship with them? How do you see your relationship with them in the future?

42. Have you ever been engaged to be married but didn't go through with the wedding?

43. Have you ever had a live-in partner? Why did you choose to live together instead of marrying? What did your experience teach you about the importance of marriage and about commitment?

44. Do you harbor fears that the person you love might reject you or fall out of love with you?

Sex

There was a time when the primary reason people got married was to have sex without guilt and shame and bear children. Without marriage, sex was taboo, and some cultures and religions still abide by the scriptural admonition "It is better to marry than to burn" (in hell for submitting to fleshly lust). I would venture to say that there is more than one way to burn. Sexual desire is one way, but so is burning with the lust that sees and uses another person's body as an object. This type of burning destroys the sacredness of expressing sexuality within the context of a committed, intimate partnership.

The issue around sexuality is living in the truth. Owning your sexuality. If you are going to be a sexual person, you need to understand what that means and accept responsibility.

Men and women tend to have different issues with owning their sexuality. For men, it is denying the significance of sex and not seeing the sacredness in the act. For women, it is more often ignorance and shame, not giving themselves permission to know what they need and then matching it with their behavior. In a conversation about your sexual expectations and fears, be sure to respect each other's boundaries. Your goal in asking these questions is not to pry into every detail of sexual history but to open a conversation about the most intimate aspect of your relationship.

45. What sexual activities do you enjoy the most? Are there specific sexual acts that make you uncomfortable? Be specific! This is no time to hedge.

46. Do you feel comfortable initiating sex? If yes, why? If no, why?

47. What do you need in order to be in the mood for sex?

48. Have you ever been sexually abused or assaulted?

49. What was the attitude toward sex in your family? Was it talked about? Who taught you about sex?

50. Do you use sex to self-medicate? If something upsets you, do you use sex to try and help you feel better?

51. Have you ever felt forced to have sex to "keep the peace"? Have you ever forced someone or been told that you forced someone to have sex with you to "keep the peace"?

52. Is sexual fidelity an absolute necessity in a good marriage?

53. Do you enjoy viewing pornography?

54. How often do you need or expect sex?

55. Have you ever had a sexual relationship with a person of the same sex?

56. Has sexual dissatisfaction ever been a factor for you in the breakup of a relationship?

Health

When you seek information about your partner's health history and practices, you are really asking, "Are you going to be there for the long haul?" and "Are you committed to being your best?" Many couples don't pay much attention to health questions until they have children or until one of them gets sick. But the issues that arise around health are primarily matters of whether you live from your wounds or from a place of wellness.

57. How would you describe the current state of your health?

58. Have you ever had a serious illness? Have you ever had surgery?

59. Do you believe it is a sacred responsibility to take care of yourself? Do you believe that taking care of your physical and mental health is a part of honoring your marriage vows?

60. Are there genetic diseases in your family or a history of cancer, heart disease, or chronic illness?

61. Do you have health insurance? Dental insurance?

62. Do you belong to a gym? If so, how much time do you spend at the gym every week?

63. Do you play sports or take exercise classes?

64. Have you ever been in a physically or emotionally abusive relationship?

65. Have you ever suffered from an eating disorder?

66. Have you ever been in a serious accident?

67. Do you take medication?

68. Have you ever had a sexually transmitted disease?

69. Have you ever been treated for a mental disorder?

70. Do you see a therapist?

71. Do you smoke, or have you ever smoked?

72. Do you consider yourself an addictive personality, and have you ever suffered from an addiction? Have you ever been told you have an addiction problem, even though you might disagree?

73. How much alcohol do you drink every week?

74. Do you use recreational drugs?

75. Do you have a medical problem that impacts your ability to have a satisfying sex life (for example, erectile dysfunction, premature ejaculation, vaginal dryness, drug/alcohol addiction, etc.)?

76. Have any of these health problems ever been a factor for you in the breakup of a relationship?

Appearance

In Chapter One, we talked about how the way a package looks doesn't provide all the information you need to know about what's inside. In a culture that places a high value on physical appearance, most people struggle with feelings of inadequacy or harbor fears that they will lose their value if they lose their looks. Trust easily breaks down when one person in a relationship is set up to feel un-attractive or when judgments about weight or age are allowed to grow out of proportion to lasting values.

77. How important is it that you always look your best?
78. How important is your spouse's appearance? Do you have strong preferences about being with a particular physical "type"?
79. Are there cosmetic procedures that you regularly undergo?
80. Is weight control important to you? Is your spouse's weight important to you? What would your reaction be if your partner were to gain a significant amount of weight?
81. How much money do you spend on clothing every year?
82. Do you worry about getting old? Do you worry about losing your looks?
83. What do you like and dislike about your appearance? When you were a child, were you often complimented or shamed about your looks?
84. What would your reaction be if your spouse lost a limb? A breast? How would you handle this loss?
85. Do you feel that you can have good chemistry with someone who is moderately physically attractive to you, or is a strong physical attraction necessary? Has physical appearance or "chemistry" ever been a factor in the breakup of a relationship?

Parenthood

Although this book is about marriage and intimate partnerships, having children is also for grown-ups, and there are all too many "adult" couples bringing children into marriages where the foundation is shaky on a good day. Being a mature adult involves recognizing that much of what you re-create in your marriage and as parents has to do with unresolved issues with your own parents and family. If you are married and don't have children yet, give them and your-self the gift of building a strong foundation before subjecting them to the chaos of parents who haven't shown up and haven't grown up.

86. Do you want children? When? How many? Are you unable to have children?

87. Would you feel unfulfilled if you were unable to have children?

88. Who is responsible for birth control? What would you do if there were an accidental pregnancy before you planned to have children?

89. What is your view of fertility treatments? Adoption? Would you adopt if you were unable to have a child naturally?

90. What is your view of abortion? Should a husband have an equal say in whether his wife has an abortion? Have you ever had an abortion?

91. Have you ever given birth to a child or fathered a child who was put up for adoption?

92. How important is it to you that your children are raised near your extended family?

93. Do you believe that a good mother will want to breast-feed her baby? Do you believe a mother or father should stay at home with a child during the first six months of life? The first year? Longer?

94. Do you believe in spanking a child? What type of discipline do you believe in (time-out, standing in the corner, taking away privileges, etc.)?

95. Do you believe that children have rights? Do you feel that a child's opinion should be considered when making family and life decisions, such as moving or changing schools?

96. Do you believe that children should be raised with some religious or spiritual foundation?

97. Should boys be treated the same as girls? Should they have the same rules for conduct? Should you have the same expectations for their sexual behavior?

98. Would you put your teenage daughter on birth control if you knew that she was sexually active?

99. How would you handle it if you didn't like your child's friends?

100. In a blended family, should birth parents be in charge of making decisions for their own children?

101. Would you ever consider getting a vasectomy or having your tubes tied? Do you believe it's your choice, or does your partner have a say?

102. Have differences concerning conception or child raising ever been a factor for you in the breakup of a relationship?

Extended Families

We all carry the imprints of our family stories, and we carry our childhood wounds into adulthood. To know another person intimately is to understand the effects of this most primary relationship.

103. Are you close to your family?

104. Are you or have you ever been alienated from your family?

105. Do you have a difficult time setting limits with family?

106. Have you identified the childhood wound that may have sabotaged your relationships in the past—the deeply imprinted fear that made you want to escape? How were you most hurt in your family, and who hurt you?

107. How important is it that you and your partner be on good terms with each other's families?

108. How did your parents settle conflicts when you were a child? Do people in your family carry long-term grudges?

109. How much influence do your parents still have over your decisions?

110. Have unresolved or ongoing family issues ever been a factor for you in the breakup of a relationship?

Friends

When we were children, our friends were our first experiment in forging our independent identities. Unlike our family members, friends are people we choose to engage with and who choose to engage with us. We perceive them, at least ideally, as people who like and admire us for who we really are. Good friendships are nonthreatening; we have permission to be honest without fear of consequences, and there is the expectation of mutual accountability. Though close friendships are a gift, many new couples struggle with the imposition of these essential others on their intimate relationship. It is important to talk about where friends will sit at your Marriage Table.

111. Do you have a "best friend"?

112. Do you see a close friend or friends at least once a week? Do you speak to any of your friends on the phone every day?

113. Are your friendships as important to you as your life partner is?

114. If your friends need you, are you there for them?

115. Is it important to you for your partner to accept and like your friends?

116. Is it important that you and your partner have friends in common?

117. Do you have a difficult time setting limits with friends?

118. Has a partner ever been responsible for breaking up a friendship? Have friends ever been a factor for you in the breakup of a relationship?

Pets

For a pet lover (and I am one), this special relationship is like no other. A pet's vulnerability and unconditional acceptance are like those of a small child; indeed, many of us slip into referring to ourselves as "Mommy" or "Daddy" when we speak to our pets. Pets can offer comfort when we are sad, companionship when we are lonely, and pure joy and friendship when we just want to run with the ball and play with reckless abandon. They can teach us to be responsible, compassionate, and caring, and they can brighten our day. This is something that people who are not pet lovers can find hard to understand; you can't convince someone who doesn't like animals that they should like them—although sometimes people do learn to love their partners' pets. Regardless of your circumstances, this subject must be explored right up front.

Few people I know love animals the way I do, and I accept this fully. But for me, the treatment of what the Bible calls "the least of these" is very important. That includes animals and children, people who live in poverty and who struggle to make ends meet, the exhausted waiter in a restaurant or the housekeeper in a hotel, someone who is mentally challenged, or the young people I work with at a local juvenile detention center. I long ago was involved with a man who was not only judgmental toward people who struggled and were less fortunate, he was also unkind to my dog. There were times when, by mistake, he would step on one of her front paws, causing her to yelp and hold her injured paw in midair. Instead of showing remorse or even concern, he would blame her for being underfoot, since she liked him and followed him around, often sticking close by his side. This was a clear sign of danger in the relationship. Not because he didn't like her but because he faulted her for being a normal, joyful dog. His inability to show remorse when he caused injury was a sign of deep deficits that would have had a major impact on our ability to create a healthy relationship. It greatly hampered my ability to feel safe with him, and it diminished my sense of trust that he could show respect to all of creation, including me. Respecting all creation didn't mean that he had to love animals or my dog in particular, but he did have to respect her as a valued member of creation and a valued treasure to me, and he had to care when he injured her. This tendency to not show remorse was pervasive throughout his life, so it wasn't about the dog; it was about who he was on the inside.

119. Are you an animal lover?

120. Do you have a dog, cat, or other beloved pet?

121. Is your attitude "Love me, love my dog [cat, potbellied pig]?"

122. Have you ever been physically aggressive with an animal? Have you deliberately hurt an animal?

123. Do you believe a person should give up his or her pet if it interferes with the relationship?

124. Do you consider pets members of your family?

125. Have you ever been jealous of a partner's relationship with a pet?

126. Have disagreements about pets ever been a factor for you in the breakup of a relationship?

Politics

Even intimate partners can have very different attitudes about social action, human rights, the role that faith plays in assuring justice for all people, and gender ideals. People often trivialize politics into party affiliation, but it's more fundamental. It's the way you view the world and your place in it. It also includes other categories of questions shown below: community, charity, the military, the law, and the media.

127. Do you consider yourself liberal, moderate, or conservative, or do you reject political labels? What was the attitude in your family about political involvement and social action?

128. Do you belong to a political party? Are you actively involved?

129. Did you vote in the last presidential election? Congressional election? Local election?

130. Do you believe that two people of differing political ideologies can have a successful marriage?

131. Do you believe that the political system is skewed against people of color, poor people, and the disenfranchised?

132. Which political issues do you care about? (For example, equality, national security, privacy, the environment, the budget, women's rights, gay rights, human rights, etc.).

133. Has politics ever been a factor in the breakup of a relationship?

Community

134. Is it important for you to be involved in your local community?

135. Do you like having a close relationship with your

neighbors? For example, would you give a neighbor a spare key to your home?

136. Do you regularly participate in community projects?

137. Do you believe that good fences make good neighbors?

138. Have you ever had a serious dispute with a neighbor?

139. Do you take pains to be considerate of your neighbors (for example, keeping a lid on loud music, barking dogs, etc.)?

Charity

140. How important is it to you to contribute time or money to charity?

141. Which kind of charities do you like to support? How much of your annual income do you donate to charity?

142. Do you feel that it is the responsibility of the "haves" of the world to help the "have nots"?

143. Have attitudes about charitable contributions ever been a factor in the breakup of a relationship?

Military

144. Have you served in the military?

145. Have your parents or other relatives served in the military?

146. Would you want your children to serve in the military?

147. Do you personally identify more with a nonviolent approach, or with making change through military force and action?

148. Has military service or attitudes about military service ever been a factor for you in the breakup of a relationship?

The Law

149. Do you consider yourself a law-abiding person?

150. Have you ever committed a crime? If yes, what was it?

151. Have you ever been arrested? If yes, for what?

152. Have you ever been in jail? If yes, why?

153. Have you ever been involved in a legal action or lawsuit? If yes, what were the circumstances?

154. Have you ever been the victim of a violent crime? If yes, describe what happened.

155. Do you believe it's important to be rigorously honest when you pay taxes?

156. Have you ever failed to pay child support? If so, why?

157. Have legal or criminal issues ever been a factor in the breakup of a relationship?

Media

158. Where do you get your news (for example, TV news programs, radio, newspapers, newsmagazines, the Internet, friends)?

159. Do you believe what you read and see in the news, or do you question where information is coming from and what the true agenda is?

160. Do you seek out media with diverse perspectives on the news?

161. Have media differences ever been a factor in the breakup of a relationship?

Religion

Like politics, religion cannot be reduced to affiliation. That's especially true today, when religion has become complicated for people. I have friends who chose not to be actively involved in a formal religion. However, she was raised as a Catholic, and he was Jewish, and these strong historical and familial influences constantly showed up as surprise guests in their lives. They thought they had rejected the religious affiliations of their parents, but when they became parents themselves, they found themselves automatically being drawn back. Naturally, this created a serious conflict about which religious influence would dominate their child's life. Because these were not dogmatic people, they eventually found a way to give their child the gift of a mixed religious heritage, but not every couple will find that possible. So when you're having a conversation about religion, open it up beyond affiliation, and find out what religion means to each of you.

162. Do you believe in God? What does that mean to you?

163. Do you have a current religious affiliation? Is it a big part of your life?

164. When you were growing up, did your family belong to a church, synagogue, temple, or mosque?

165. Do you currently practice a different religion from the one in which you were raised?

166. Do you believe in life after death?

167. Does your religion impose any behavioral restrictions (dietary, social, familial, sexual) that would affect your partner?

168. Do you consider yourself a religious person? A spiritual person?

169. Do you engage in spiritual practices outside of organized religion?

170. How important is it to you for your partner to share your religious beliefs?

171. How important is it to you for your children to be raised in your religion?

172. Is spirituality a part of your daily life and practice?

173. Has religion or spiritual practice ever been a factor in the breakup of a relationship?

Culture

We cannot escape popular culture. It is all around us, and its influence is as pervasive as the air we breathe. Sometimes it elevates and enriches us. Other times it depresses us to the point that we question our assumptions about human intelligence and soul. Individual preferences play a big part in our attitudes about culture, and partners can live happily with different preferences. I know a woman who takes weekly tango lessons with friends while her husband attends art movies. They're content with their separate interests. On the other hand, I've known people whose obsessions with popular culture became an alienating factor in their relationships. Personal obsessions always create barriers to intimacy. These considerations also involve your attitudes and behaviors around leisure time.

How driven are you to look good in the eyes of others? Are you your own barometer, or do you weigh everything against what your family, friends, cultural icons, or Hollywood movie stars are doing? How much of your life is rooted in what you value, and where are your values coming from?

174. Does popular culture have an important impact on your life?

175. Do you spend time reading about, watching, or discussing actors, musicians, models, or other celebrities?

176. Do you think most celebrities have a better, more exciting life than you do? (By the way, if they do, maybe it's because they are living their lives, while you are *watching* them live their lives. Are you wasting the opportunity and gift to live your own life?)

177. Do you regularly go to the movies, or do you prefer to rent movies and watch them at home?

178. What is your favorite style of music?

179. Do you attend concerts featuring your favorite musicians?

180. Do you enjoy going to museums or art shows?

181. Do you like to dance?

182. Do you like to watch TV for entertainment?

183. Have attitudes or behaviors around popular culture ever been a factor in the breakup of a relationship?

Leisure

184. What is your idea of a fun day?

185. Do you have a hobby that's important to you?

186. Do you enjoy spectator sports?

187. Are certain seasons off-limits for other activities because of football, baseball, basketball, or other sports?

188. What activities do you enjoy that don't involve your partner? How important is it to you that you and your partner enjoy the same leisure activities?

189. How much money do you regularly spend on leisure activities?

190. Do you enjoy activities that might make your partner uncomfortable, such as hanging out in bars drinking, going to strip clubs, or gambling?

191. Have leisure time issues ever been a factor in the breakup of a relationship?

Social Life

I've seen marriages break up over the inability to reach consensus when one person is social and the other is not. Seemingly frivolous issues have deeper roots related to how we see ourselves in the world, what we take and what we give, and our sense of ourselves as acceptable and cherished by others. It can be true that a person who needs frequent social engagements is looking for a constant confirmation of being okay in the eyes of the world. Conversely, a person who is overly resistant to social engagements usually has a fear of being rejected. Social people are likely to mate with less social people, each looking for that missing piece of themselves in the other. The goal in a grown-up relationship is to achieve a healthy balance, and to engage socially from a place of confidence, while still finding space to nurture yourself and your relationship.

The same distinctions are also true of differing ideas about celebrating holidays or special occasions and planning vacations. In a grown-up relationship, there will be a collaboration to create something that is, while not perfect, at least acceptable and respectful to both partners.

This is where you practice sharing power, which means respecting that your partner is not the same person as you and has a different way of finding joy and pleasure. When I hear someone say that his or her partner won't go to a movie because "I don't like action films" or "I don't like chick flicks," my response is always the same: "So what? This isn't about what type of movie you like, it's about whether or not you want to be generous in your relationship." When we take the position that we won't do things because they aren't what we personally enjoy the most, it's just self-centered, and narrows the path on which intimacy travels. I will tell you the truth about good marriages: *People do things that don't particularly float their boats because it's good for the relationship.* This is called maturity, and it leads to healthy, happy marriages.

192. Do you enjoy entertaining, or do you worry that you'll do something wrong or people won't have a good time?

193. Is it important for you to attend social events regularly, or does the prospect rarely appeal to you?

194. Do you look forward to at least one night out every week, or do you prefer to enjoy yourself at home?

195. Does your work involve attending social functions? If so, are these occasions a burden or a pleasure? Do you expect your spouse to be present, or do you prefer that your spouse not be present?

196. Do you socialize primarily with people from work, or with people from the same ethnic/racial/religious/ socioeconomic background? Or do you socialize with a diverse mix of people?

197. Are you usually the "life of the party," or do you dislike being singled out for attention?

198. Have you or a partner ever had an argument caused by one or the other's behavior at a social function?

199. Have differences about socializing ever been a factor for you in the breakup of a relationship?

Holidays and Birthdays

200. Which (if any) holidays do you believe are the most important to celebrate?

201. Do you maintain a family tradition around certain holidays?

202. How important are birthday celebrations to you? Anniversaries?

203. Have differences about holidays/birthdays ever been a factor for you in the breakup of a relationship?

Travel/Vacations

204. Do you enjoy traveling, or are you a homebody?

205. Are vacation getaways an important part of your yearly planning?

206. How much of your annual income do you designate for vacation and travel expenses?

207. Do you have favorite vacation destinations? Do you believe it's wasteful to spend money on vacations to distant places?

208. Do you think it's important to have a passport? To speak a foreign language?

209. Have disputes about travel and vacation ever been a factor in the breakup of a relationship?

Education

Education is the sleeping dog in many relationships. Our attitudes are so deeply ingrained that we may not even realize we have them. Yet differences in education level, and the amount of importance given to continuing education, arise when there are other power struggles in the relationship. Openness to learning can be a clue about your partner's openness in other areas.

210. What is your level of formal education? Is your education a source of pride or shame?

211. Do you regularly sign up for courses that interest you, or enroll in advanced-learning programs that will help you in your career or profession?

212. Do you think that college graduates are smarter than people who didn't attend college? Have disparities in education ever been a source of tension for you in a relationship, or ended a relationship?

213. How do you feel about private school education for children? Do you have a limit on how much you would be willing to invest in private school education?

214. Have education levels or priorities ever been a factor in the breakup of a relationship?

Transportation

We live in a society where cars are symbols of identity and independence. For many people, they are an important way to claim personal space in the world. Others view their cars as a necessary evil. Which are you? Which is your partner?

215. Do you own or lease a car? Would you ever consider not having a car?

216. Is the year, make, and model of the car you drive important to you? Is your car your "castle"?

217. Are fuel efficiency and environmental protection factors when you choose a car?

218. Given the availability of reliable public transportation, would you prefer not to drive a car at all?

219. How much time do you spend maintaining and caring for your vehicle? Are you reluctant to let others drive your car?

220. How long is your daily commute? Is it by bus, train, car, carpool?

221. Do you consider yourself a good driver? Have you ever received a speeding ticket?

222. Have cars or driving ever been a factor in the breakup of a relationship?

Communication

I somehow doubt that before the invention of the telephone, people felt threatened or annoyed because their partners were "always writing letters." Today, with the advent of cell phones and Black-Berrys, it is possible to always be on the phone, e-mail, or in communication with someone. This can rightfully cause conflicts in relationships, especially when your partner believes that a ringing phone takes precedence over the living being in front of him or her.

223. How much time do you spend on the phone every day?

224. Do you have a cell phone? A BlackBerry?

225. Do you belong to any Internet chat groups? Do you spend significant time each day writing e-mails?

226. Do you have an unlisted telephone number? If yes, why?

227. Do you consider yourself a communicator or a private person?

228. What are the circumstances under which you would *not* answer the telephone, cell phone, or BlackBerry?

229. Has modern communication ever been a factor in the breakup of a relationship?

Mealtime

If the sole purpose of food were nutrition, by now we probably would have figured out a way to condense it to a daily capsule. Obviously, it means much, much more than that. What we eat, when we eat, where we eat, the people with whom we eat, and how much significance we place on all of the above are a big deal.

230. Do you like to eat most of your meals sitting at the table, or do you tend to eat on the run?

231. Do you love to cook? Do you love to eat?

232. When you were growing up, was it important that everybody be present for dinner?

233. Do you follow a specific diet regimen that limits your food choices? Do you expect others in your household to adhere to certain dietary restrictions?

234. In your family, is food ever used as a bribe or a proof of love?

235. Has eating ever been a source of shame for you?

236. Have eating and food ever been a source of tension and stress in a relationship? Have they ever been a factor in the breakup of a relationship?

Gender Roles

We strive for equality in our relationships, but we carry within us the powerful influences of childhood, which is where we learned to model gender roles. Sometimes our assumptions about who does what are so buried that we don't know we have them until they start getting acted out. The challenge for couples today is to divest themselves of models that don't work, and invest in models that reflect their beliefs and commitment. Gender stereotypes are so ingrained by society, family, religion, and the media that intentionally challenging false role ideals is one of the most important gifts you can give yourself and your partner.

237. Are there household responsibilities you believe to be the sole domain of a man or a woman? Why do you believe this?
238. Do you believe that marriages are stronger if a woman defers to her husband in most areas? Do you need to feel either in control or taken care of?
239. How important is equality in a marriage? Define what you mean by "equality."
240. Do you believe that roles in your family should be filled by the person best equipped for the job, even if it is an unconventional arrangement?
241. How did your family view the roles of girls and boys, men and women? In your family, could anyone do any job as long as it got done well?
242. Have different ideas about gender roles ever been a source of tension for you in a relationship, or the cause of a breakup?

Race, Ethnicity, and Differences

America is still living a separate, unequal existence as it relates to race and ethnicity, but we have chosen to hit the snooze button on the impact this has on us as a nation. It is extremely important to explore how this blind spot can show up in marriage as an unexpected guest at the Marriage Table. Issues of race and ethnicity can reach a boiling point quickly, but facing the issues truthfully can lead to a deeper understanding of yourself and your partner, increasing your level of intimacy.

243. What did you learn about race and ethnic differences as a child?
244. Which of those beliefs from childhood do you still carry, and which have you shed?

245. Does your work environment look more like the United Nations, or like a mirror of yourself? How about your personal life?

246. How would you feel if your child dated someone of a different race or ethnicity? The same gender? How would you feel if he or she married this person?

247. Are you aware of your own biases regarding race and ethnicity? What are they? Where did they come from? (We aren't born biased, we learn it, and it's important to trace where it was learned.)

248. Have race, ethnicity, and differences ever been a source of tension and stress for you in a relationship?

249. What were your family's views of race, ethnicity, and difference?

250. Is it important to you that your partner share your vision of race, ethnicity, and difference?

251. Have different ideas about race, ethnicity, and difference ever been a factor in the breakup of a relationship?

Living Every Day

As the saying goes, life happens when you're busy doing other things. Marriages are made or broken on daily interactions. These are small questions with a big impact.

252. Would you consider yourself a morning person or a night person?

253. Do you judge people who have a different waking and sleeping clock than you?

254. Are you a physically affectionate person?

255. What is your favorite season of the year?

256. When you disagree with your partner, do you tend to fight or withdraw?

257. What is your idea of a fair division of labor in your household?

258. Do you consider yourself an easygoing person, or are you most comfortable with a firm plan of action?

259. How much sleep do you need every night?

260. Do you like to be freshly showered and wearing clean clothes every day, even on weekends or vacations?

261. What is your idea of perfect relaxation?

262. What makes you really angry? What do you do when you're really angry?

263. What makes you most joyful? What do you do when you are joyful?

264. What makes you most insecure? How do you handle your insecurities?

265. What makes you most secure?

266. Do you fight fair? How do you know?

267. How do you celebrate when something great happens? How do you mourn when something tragic happens?

268. What is your greatest limitation?

269. What is your greatest strength?

270. What most stands in the way of your creating a passionate and caring marriage?

271. What do you need to do today to move toward making your dream marriage a reality?

272. What makes you most afraid?

273. What drains you of your joy and passion?

274. What replenishes your mind, body, and spirit?

275. What makes your heart smile in tough times?

276. What makes you feel the most alive?

These conversations should certainly take place before marriage, but they are also conversations for a lifetime. Revisit them as you grow together or when you're struggling with a particular issue in your marriage. Take them to another level to clear the old brush. Continue to rewrite your scripts to make your life your own.

Adopt the "No Surprises" rule. You can't be prepared for everything, but you can break the silence that has crippled past generations of married couples. Remember, it is a lie that it's better to wait until later—after the wedding, after the first year of marriage, after the children are born, after the children are grown, after retirement—to find out what you're all about. If you wait, life will pass you by.

Take courage today, and begin the discussion. Don't overwhelm yourself or your partner. This is a place to begin creating the foundation for a satisfying and loving union that will last a lifetime. These questions are just a guide. Use them as a springboard and add the questions that are near and dear to your heart, mind, and spirit.

Ten

How to Write True Vows to Live By

Your wedding day is approaching. You have the location reserved, a historic mansion you had to book two years in advance. The invitations you spent hours fretting over were sent weeks ago. The menu is set—a catered dinner for two hundred of your nearest and dearest, with an entrée choice of prime rib or sea bass. The hottest wedding band around has been hired. The color scheme has been chosen. The rings have been purchased. The cake has been ordered—a five-tiered creation draped in edible pearls and hydrangea blossoms that cost a pretty penny. The bouquets and flower arrangements have been ordered. The one-of-a-kind wedding dress and the gowns for the four bridesmaids, the maid of honor, and the twin flower girls have been purchased and fitted to perfection. Tuxedoes have been rented and altered for the groom, the best man, and the four groomsmen. The stretch limos have been booked and are ready to roll. The honeymoon arrangements have been finalized and set. The shower was held on schedule four weeks ago and was a smashing success. Bachelor and bachelorette parties have been arranged. The grand event is just two weeks away.

What else is there left to do? Oh, yes, it's time to think about the wedding ceremony.

I've known many couples who were handed a copy of their

vows for the first time at their wedding rehearsal, a formulaic "repeat after me" script. I've also seen couples frantically searching at the last minute for someone to officiate, because neither of them belonged to a congregation or church. Lots of people accept the local clergyperson or officiant who is tacked on as part of a package deal with the destination wedding site. They meet the person who will join them in holy matrimony for the *first time* the day before the wedding ceremony is to take place. Relieved to have a warm body to fill the role, they don't seem to mind that they're getting a canned service and sermon from a stranger who doesn't know them from Adam and Eve.

Of course, many people are just as happy being married by the local judge, village clerk, or justice of the peace, even at a Las Vegas wedding chapel complete with an Elvis impersonator presiding over the ceremony; the point being, they are getting married. Some people are looking to add a little eccentricity and spice, a little joie de vivre, to their wedding day—it's all part of the fun, and it doesn't cost an arm and a leg.

There is no right or wrong way to have a wedding. I would like to raise the possibility, however, that once you have decided to show up as grown-ups, you have the opportunity to plan a wedding that reflects your intention.

The wedding-planner industry isn't going to love me for saying it, but I think we've lost the heart and soul of the wedding amid the emphasis on everything but the sacredness of the vows. The ceremony too often becomes an afterthought to the big party that follows. And we wonder why so many couples get the post-wedding blues, as if the wedding were an ending, not a beginning.

Perhaps that is why so many brides, and perhaps some grooms, suffer from post-traumatic wedding disorder. The letdown is enormous. All of that furious planning and organizing, the forces marshaled and the money spent, *all of that attention,* and then what? Well, the honeymoon is over, literally and figuratively. Reality once again bangs you in the face, and there you are, back in day-to-day life. The two of you are husband and wife at last. Left alone together to begin your married life, filled with connubial bliss. Or are you? For some people, it's a gray and depressing experience. Where has all of the excitement gone, all of the magic? What happened? What happens now?

What has happened is very clear. Many people lose sight of the magnificence of the ritual itself. It is absurd to think that you can plan a wedding for two years, giving little thought to your marriage, and then think that somehow, magically, everything will work out fine. That is a lie, it is fantasy, and it is the thief that will steal your happiness every time. I invite you to consider bringing intention and meaning back into your big day. Restore your vows to their proper place as the centerpiece of your wedding, a meaningful prelude to the life you want to live together. I believe you *can* have it all—the trappings of elegance wrapped in the meaning of vows to live by.

THE WEDDING RITUAL

Occasionally, I am given the gift of being witness to some beautiful moments. I have assisted in performing wedding ceremonies for couples who wanted to include words about living in an awakened marriage. Recently, I was a guest at a dear friend's wedding. She is a wonderful woman; we have known each other since childhood, our parents were dear friends, and we've weathered many seasons of love and loss together. She had waited many years for the "right" man to appear—one that honored her beauty, brains—she's very smart—and her spiritual clarity. Getting married to a mediocre man wasn't going to satisfy her. She chose to live alone rather than compromise. It had been a long and arduous journey for her to create a deep and lasting love in her life. Although her wedding ceremony employed the traditional vows, what I so loved about it was the role that her pastor chose to play. He didn't just say the words and ask the couple to repeat after him. Instead, he used the opportunity to include the bride and groom and the entire congregation in a conversation about the meaning of the vows. Although I was one of the honored guests, I discreetly took a pen and paper from my purse and wrote down a few of the pastor's words on the wedding program. "Marriage is not about manipulation or domination," he quietly exhorted. "Nor is it about slavery, one serving the other as if in bondage. No. Marriage is a covenant between equals. Marriage is not a covenant between competitors. Marriage is a bond of love, and there is a huge difference between love and lust." I admired the way the pastor made the wedding ceremony resonate with its true meaning. He was clear that marriage is about emotional and spiritual maturity, about adults expressing the strength of their union.

In choosing him to officiate, this couple showed that they were entering marriage with wisdom and maturity. It was an exhilarating experience—a traditional ceremony, with the traditional vows incorporating and illuminating the truth about what the bride and groom were saying "yes" and "I do" to. I left the wedding and reception knowing that I had just witnessed the real deal. That day I was blessed to gaze upon love, truth, commitment, passion, joy, and devotion at their best. There was no illusion of the pursuit of wedding or marital perfection. It wasn't necessary, because the reality was far more beautiful and intoxicating than any fantasy wedding ceremony could ever be. I was changed and challenged as I witnessed this high level of showing up and growing up. I believe this is what most people want when they say "I do." They just have no idea how to define it, or how to find the road that takes them there. By the way, my friend did it all. A ceremony full of meaning, love, joy, and accountability, followed by a fabulous reception overlooking a beautiful body of water, with boats, people, and great food. The sun fully shined on her celebration of love.

A ritual should stir the deepest part of us, awaken our sense of wonder and awe to the greater powers that rule our most primal beliefs. To come before our gathered family and friends and vow to love, honor, and cherish one another is not a moment to be taken lightly.

THE VOWS

You've decided to write your own vows, because you want them to have special personal meaning. Where to begin? You start surfing the Web and discover hundreds of sites—a treasure trove of romantic poetry, sentimental thoughts, scriptural quotes, moving song lyrics, and fill-in-the-blank formulas. You cobble them together, selecting those that bring tears to your eyes, the magnificent promises of a lifetime. You say, "Oh, honey, that's so beautiful." You bask in the land of everlasting love. You cling to the lyrics of "your" song, as if it will keep you aloft through all the days to come.

The question to ask yourself is whether you add meaning to your vows by replacing the more traditional phrases with self-selected poetry, sentimental notions, or song lyrics.

Many couples approach writing personalized vows the same way they choose a personalized wedding bouquet or the wedding cake. Personally chosen vows can sound beautiful and make both of you feel good on your special day, but they're often easily forgotten, as ephemeral as freshly whipped cream. Six months down the road, will one of you turn to the other and say, "Hey, didn't you promise to always turn my life on with a smile?"

I conducted a little experiment, asking people if they had written their own vows. Most of them said yes. I then asked if they remembered them, and almost everyone admitted they did not, including one person who had been married under two years. The words, though carefully chosen, had not left a mark. This could happen only because the focus was on the details of the wedding and not on the sacred commitment being made to each other.

Wedding vows are the centerpiece of a ritualized intention. The intention is to set out together on a lifelong journey—to take the words spoken as vows during the ritual and make them come fully alive each and every day. In this book, I've used traditional phrasing as a template. But it's the meaning resonating beneath the words and phrases that truly matters.

Begin by reviewing the work you've already done while reading this book. Take another look at all of the exercises you've worked through. Your answers are the building blocks of your future. They are your truth.

Your task is to choose the thoughts that reflect that truth. (By the time you are writing wedding vows, you should know that you share the same truth, the same vision, and the same purpose.) The vows you speak are the public manifestation of a private promise. Part of this task is to figure out how you're going to make your vows mean something so profound to both of you that they will constantly ring true and come alive while you're busy living your real, everyday life. And that you will use them as an anchor when your marital ship has drifted off course.

Marriage is a human institution that calls upon us to accept our humanity while striving to transform its limitations. In that spirit, let me suggest that your vows include four elements:

1. **Intentional vows state your truths.** These are your core beliefs and commitments, grounded in reality.

2. **Intentional vows reflect the acceptance of your and your partner's individuality and needs.** This is your promise to witness the other as he or she is, to perform acts of love, to share yourself, and to support your partner's best self.

3. **Intentional vows acknowledge the brokenness and possibility of life.** This is the promise to help each other up when you fall, to hold each other accountable with respect, dignity, and compassion, and to always look for the possibility in life for opportunities to repair what is broken.

4. **Intentional vows embrace the world around you.** This is your commitment to share your hearts with families, friends, and the wider community.

Intentional vows reinforce your core values in living words. What do I mean by "living words"? I mean words you can picture in reality. For example, to say "I will love you for all eternity" sounds lovely, but it is not a promise you can keep.

The following is an example of living vows:

I promise . . .
To seek the truth when tempted by lies.
To stay present when I want to turn away.
To choose compassion when anger feels easier.

To embrace your needs and care about them like my own.
To give and receive comfort during hard times.
To share my heart with those you love.
To make your family people that I care about because you do.
To nurture you with honesty, joy, and passion.
To grow with you.
To be a witness to your life and invite you to be a witness to mine.

These are extremely moving statements because they are grounded in truth; they speak to your and your partner's individuality and needs; they accept the brokenness of life as well as its possibility; and they embrace a larger world than just your union.

Using the four elements of intentional vows, you can begin to craft your vows as your own. This is just a formula to help you get started.

I promise to [state your truth]_____,
to [accept your and my individuality and needs]_____,
to [acknowledge our brokenness and possibility]_____,
to [embrace the world around us]_____.

Ritualize Your Vows in Life

How do you make your vows live inside of you? The simple answer is that you practice them, living the truth of your commitment daily. Marriage is a lifelong journey, but it is not meant to be a lifelong struggle. In fact, it can get easier, the love deeper, the passion sweeter. With time and practice, habits form that make what was once a difficulty second nature—as long as the habits you form enhance you. People learn to play the piano by practicing, to speak a foreign language by using the language as much as possible, to play a sport by training. I once heard Michael Jordan say that for all the shots he made, there were many more that he missed while he was practicing. He kept shooting until the number of balls going into the basket exceeded the number of balls hitting the rim and bouncing off. It's the same with marriage. It takes practice, determination, commitment, and focus. Remember my marital ATM analogy: what you put in is what you get out—nothing more, nothing less. You can't make withdrawals when you haven't make deposits.

Wedding vows are not magical oaths. Saying you love, honor, and cherish someone doesn't necessarily make it so. Couples have to grow into their vows by intentionally finding ways to turn them into concrete, loving actions.

Once you have written your vows, choose a daily practice that will be a manifestation of your intention. Note that these practices will grow and change as your marriage grows and changes. For now the goal is to cement your vow with an action.

You can practice living your vows by establishing rituals. The important thing about rituals is that they transcend feelings. You already know this from life. Maybe you haven't felt like getting up and attending your weekly religious service, but you've gone anyway. Maybe you haven't felt like going to the gym, but you've gone anyway. I know there are times when you haven't felt like going to work or completing a project, but you've done it anyway. Intentional rituals force you to be present when you want to exit; they enable you to be your better self even when your tank is running low.

Your rituals can be any actions you choose that reflect the spirit and substance of your vows. Here are some examples:

- A couple I know takes turns each Saturday evening at the end of their Sabbath to plan something that they really want to do and share with each other. It's important to do things that your partner enjoys. It is a great reminder that the whole world does not revolve around you, and it beats back the human tendency to be self-absorbed. (And next week it's your turn.)
- Many couples choose simple rituals that cultivate loving-kindness and a level of thoughtfulness that heal relationships and fuel passionate connections. These include never leaving the house in the morning without saying "I love you"; greeting each other in the evening with a hug, a kiss, and a

"How was your day?" (and wanting to hear the answer); and turning off the phones one evening a week as a time just for you.

• Intentional actions that change your behavior to benefit your partner can be particularly potent. One idea is to practice responding with a "yes" to requests your partner makes. This is surprisingly possible—and effective. Here's an example:

NO refrain:
"Honey, could you put out the garbage?"
"Not right now. I'm busy."
YES refrain:
"Honey, could you put out the garbage?"
"Okay, sure, as soon as I'm finished with this article."

If you look carefully, the words above say the same thing, which is "I'll do it," but they hit the heart of your partner in different ways. The first is closed and harsh, the second caring, respectful, and responsive. You can learn to be smart with your words.

Think about how you can use intentional actions to change behaviors that you know bug your partner. For example, decide you're not going to get into a political argument with your mother-in-law when you see her this week, or perform an errand your partner usually takes care of.

You might devise an argument ritual to replace the meaningless dictums floating around in your head ("Fight fair" or "Never go to sleep angry"). For example, when you have a disagreement, before it turns into a full-fledged battle of intractable positions, stop and do a form of mirroring that involves each of you writing down the other person's position as a statement. Not "She thinks we should buy a new car because . . ." but "We should buy a new car because . . ." This exercise arms you with each other's viewpoints, encourages listening, and helps create a deeper understanding. When you feel seen and heard, it's an invitation to deep passion, intimacy, and devotion.

Who Will Officiate?

Earlier, I told the story of my friend's wedding because it impressed upon me how important it is to choose an officiant who reflects your values. It baffles me why a couple would spend more time and effort choosing a band for their reception than choosing the individual who officiates at their wedding ceremony.

Couples who aren't members of religious congregations, or are of different faiths, often struggle with finding a clergyperson to preside over the religious aspects of the wedding ceremony. Although this custom seems to be slowly changing, relatively few clergy are willing or able to preside over interfaith weddings or weddings of couples who are not in their congregations.

Don't settle for an officiant or a setting that does not fully affirm your union. A man who was very close to me was getting remarried. He had been divorced for quite some time and had finally found the fulfillment and joy of grounded and passionate love. He was so excited about his big day, and I shared in his joy for a second chance at love. He and his fiancée had a pastor who was excited about uniting this couple in marriage. There was only one problem: This couple's church had been destroyed by fire and their new sanctuary wasn't going to be ready in time for their wedding ceremony. They found a local church in their community that met their needs in terms of style and location. However, when they approached the pastor about using his sanctuary for their ceremony, he expressed concerns because my friend was divorced. This great and promising couple quickly decided that they didn't want to hold their special day in a church that did not fully affirm and celebrate them and the second chance that God had given them. They withdrew their request and found a better location, an even more beautiful sanctuary, and a pastor who was happy to open the doors of his church to house this celebration of love. They understood that while all of the details of the wedding were important and they wanted everyone to enjoy their reception, where they held the ceremony, the person who performed it, and the words that they proclaimed that day were all hallowed and sacred.

The mad scramble to locate an official belies the true importance of the individual who is such a vital member of your wedding experience. Whomever you choose will be remembered forever as your representative before the community who gathers for your ceremony. Ask yourselves:

Which person can best sanctify our special day?
Who can best interpret our purpose and our values?
Who can work with us on creating our own unique vows, and help us elevate our ceremony into something meaningful and purpose-driven?
Who can encourage us to take our goals to the next level and make them concrete?
Who honors us and celebrates our joy?

These are crucial questions. If you don't have a congregation, or the clergy of your congregation doesn't match your common values, you have the right to interview others to find the individual who can best help to ritualize your union.

Don't cheat yourself. Take the time to find someone who can walk with you—not just through the choice of cakes, flowers, your color palette, the reception location, the photographer, videographer, guest list, rehearsal dinners, and the full laundry list of wedding-day necessities. Choose someone who cares about your life after the wedding, about your joys and sorrows. If you're going to shop till you drop for something, then make it a person who signifies that your wedding day is more than a grand party, that it is more than a day to impress the world with a show of your resources. It is a day to show yourself, your partner, and your witnesses that you are creating a marriage that is the envy of all, not just a *wedding* that is the envy of all.

In the Presence of the Community

There is an important reason that weddings are performed in the presence of the community, be it a roomful of people or two designated witnesses. We don't just sign a marriage certificate at the county clerk's office and walk away married.

Think about your community—family, friends, colleagues, neighbors, and so on—and imagine how you might open yourselves to these people who know you and want the best for you. How can you make your wedding an opportunity to give and receive wisdom and inspiration?

Here are a couple of suggestions.

The Shower of Wisdom

Standard bridal showers focus on the externals. There are lingerie showers, kitchen showers, honeymoon travel showers, beauty and spa showers, and dozens of others. One friend suggested throwing a Shower of Wisdom for the bride, and it became a truly inspired occasion. Don't worry. I'm not saying you have to forgo the material gifts if you want to make them a part of the event, because that can be fun, too. But use the gathering for friends to impart wisdom. My friend tape-recorded the event and presented the bride with a bound book containing the transcripts of the advice. Ask each person to do one of the following:

- Tell a story from her own marriage (or one she observed) that taught her a valuable lesson she is now imparting.
- Read a passage from a book or a poem to reflect on during times of struggle.

As every woman knows, our friends are wise in ways that enhance our lives and seem necessary to our very survival. The Shower of Wisdom has the added benefit of providing inspiration to everyone in the room. The whole village benefits from it.

The Giving and Receiving Line

Now ask: What would it mean to create a wedding experience for your guests that lasts beyond the ceremony and reception?

Your family and friends are not just warm bodies to fill the pews on both sides of the church. Nor is it their primary role to set your table and fill your kitchen with the patterns from bridal registries. In addition to receiving from them, you can give them something worthwhile to take away—a wedding in which everybody participates, in both spirit and reality. By creating a day that invites your guests to be more than bystanders, you can give them a gift, too. Imagine how remarkable it would be if every one of your wedding guests left having experienced love, truth, and possibility—not just for your life, but for themselves as well.

Eleven

It's Never Too Late
to Renew Your Vows

A long-married friend wistfully confessed to me, "How I wish I could recapture that magical feeling of sheer hope and expectation that I felt on my wedding day." My friend had enjoyed a strong marriage, but the passage of years had worn away its luster, and the union felt stale and weathered to her. As she looked back from the vantage point of twenty-two years later, her wedding day shimmered in her memory with a vivacity and joy that seemed impossible to recover.

In one sense, she was right. The vigor and vibrancy of youth, the splendor of its fleeting beauty, cannot be restored once the decades have engraved their relentless imprint. However, what my friend didn't realize was that the collective lessons of the years create their own exciting potential for those willing to recognize them.

Anything is possible in a marriage where you both commit to being awake and fully present. Even if you were lying at the altar on your wedding day, and your marriage has been marked by more struggle than joy, there is redemption in the truth.

If you are already married, you may have felt a spark of recognition as you've read. You may have felt sadness at seeing the ways in which you have placed lies like boulders in your path. You may feel that it's too late to have the marriage you really want—that your flawed behaviors are cemented by years of repetition.

But I want you to know that renewing your vows does not mean that you have to undo all the bad stuff. You don't have to go back and do battle with every problem, resolve every conflict in order to move on. You don't have to excavate every "he said this" or "she said that" injury of the past thirty years. Learning from the past does not mean marinating in it. It means being aware of the influences that shaped you from the beginning; being grounded in the truth of your life and choosing possibility and new life over complacency and defeat.

Maybe you didn't show up for twenty-five years, but you're showing up today. Let's reconstruct from today.

RENEWAL IN TRUTH

After thirty years of marriage, Anna and Franklin had come to live separate lives. Their two children were grown and had moved out of the house. Anna was often away on business, but even when she was home, she rarely saw Franklin, whose job as a youth director for a local community center consumed most of his time. They had lost the desire to be together. The energy had drained out of their marriage, along with the memory of what had once drawn them together so powerfully.

The realization that they were in crisis was deeply troubling to Anna. As she looked desperately for a lifeline, their pastor suggested that they renew their vows as a way of restoring a sense of commitment to their marriage. And so, in a private ceremony at the altar of their church, Anna and Franklin stood before their pastor and restated their promise to love, honor, and cherish each other until death. Afterward, they walked hand in hand out into the sunny afternoon, feeling in that moment a surge of hope.

Two months later, they separated. A year later, they were divorced. What happened?

What Anna and Franklin were renewing was not their vows

but the lie that had placed them in crisis in the first place. It was a lie that a ceremony of renewal could *create* renewal, when they didn't understand what was broken in the first place. It was a lie that a commitment to "try harder" meant anything but doing what they had always done—the same isolating schedules, the constant sabotaging of events meant to draw them closer together, and the same old destructive behaviors. One definition of insanity is doing the same thing over and over, expecting a different result.

I have no doubt that Anna and Franklin *wanted* to save their marriage. They *wanted* things to work out. But you cannot *wish* a marriage into changing. You cannot fix a marriage if you don't have a clue what went into breaking it. You cannot fulfill a promise with blind hope. The Bible says, "Faith without works is dead." I give the following example in keynote addresses: You can't put the exercise video on in the morning, then get back in the bed and watch someone else do the work, thinking you're going to have tighter abs, a flatter stomach, and firmer thighs. You must do the work to reap the benefits.

Hope without action is of no real use. It's just another way of staying stuck in a rut. It's a dead end. When hope is the basis of a relationship, instead of feet-on-the-ground reality, there *is* no relationship. The word "hope" can be like the word "try." They are the words people use when they are actually planning a way out of doing the necessary work to repair and grow a relationship. Most of the time, when we say we're going to try, we are already setting up our justifications for failure.

Anna and Franklin believed they could rebuild their marriage while remaining in the isolation of their frightened childhood selves. They pretended to be adults by wearing adult clothes, working adult jobs, and taking on the adult responsibilities of raising kids, but beneath it all, they remained the same walking-wounded children who had never grown up. The promise of adult love had eluded them.

Rituals have meaning only if they represent truth. The ceremony to renew your vows can hold great possibility, but only if you show up as adults and rewrite the original script. Renewing your vows with truth as your goal allows you to face each other and be the best selves that you are today.

YOUR BROKENNESS CAN MAKE YOU WHOLE

A powerful story in the New Testament tells of the apostle Paul being shipwrecked at sea. A hurricane rose up without warning and crushed the vessel, flinging many on board into the turbulent waters. But in the storm-tossed sea, some of them managed to hold on to flotsam and jetsam and floated to shore on the broken pieces of the ship. I have often used this story in seminars to point out that what we may think of as hopelessly broken can still bring us to safety and aliveness. We may believe that we are drowning, that we are lost at sea, but help comes in many forms. What seems broken can sometimes be transformed into a life raft that brings us safely to shore and back to life.

So I invite you to take the shards of your marriage and make them your life raft, your teacher. Examining them will help you understand the lies you have lived with, and assist you in creating new marriage vows based on the truth. Maybe you thought forsaking all others meant living in an isolated cocoon, and you discovered long ago that was a lie. Use that knowledge to forgive yourself and your partner for the ways in which you have each colluded in stealing precious opportunities to heal and grow. But that was then, and this is now. Oprah Winfrey often quotes her treasured mentor and dear friend, Dr. Maya Angelou, who said, "You do better when you know better." So now that you know better, be wise, let courage take you by the hand, and let truth be the belt that holds your life together.

As for my friend who recounted wistful memories of her youthful fantasies, it is hard to acknowledge the broken pieces of a long marriage. We all wish that our lives could evolve out of one great and good thing after another, but things don't usually work out that way. Instead, the profound hardships—the bad times that have honed, chiseled, and processed us—teach us how to truly live, if we let them.

Remember Dr. Harville Hendrix's notion that your partner holds the blueprint for your healing? When there is safety, trust, and respect in the relationship, your partner can help you see the areas that are cheating you of the rich destiny that every person desires and deserves. When couples run away from what I call their "hot spots," they're in trouble. The hot spots are the issues that feel supercharged with emotion. If they're left untreated, the heat of resentment is likely to burn a hole in the relationship eventually and make it irreparable. When that happens, affairs, infidelity, as well as other forms of relationship exits seem like a rescue from the repellent heat. This is another huge lie. They are cheap substitutes and you can never heal an original and sacred wound with an artificial substitute. The Universe won't allow that. It's the cheap way out, and ultimately you will lose each time.

Hot spots in the life of a couple highlight the areas that are necessary for the growth of the individual. It is the responsibility of each individual to deal with his or her problems and issues and in turn bring a more mature self to bear in order to positively impact the growth of the relationship. To do otherwise is to remain in a perpetual state of misery and denial, living your lives as two people alone in the same space.

Marriage is never easy. Two individuals cannot expect to be of one mind and one feeling in every instance. That is a fantasy. However, when the differences threaten the stability of what you have built together, it is time to pause and take another look at your common values. Life rolls boulders of contention into your path, blocking the way to accord. That is a given. It's what you will do then that determines your destiny. The boulders that show up on your life's path are there to teach you something about yourself. As each one appears, ask, "What is this boulder in my life to teach me?" As you receive the gift and learn the lesson, you will watch the boulders roll away, and ultimately be grateful for the lesson it brought, tailor made for your specific needs. But for this process to occur, you must embrace the truth and all the information it brings.

RENEWING YOUR VOWS

The concept of renewing a covenant is a primary theme of the Old Testament. God renewed His covenant with the Israelites even when some had fallen into sin, pronouncing the eternal promise of redemption. He lifted them up with a new covenant as a sign of His forgiveness for their past transgressions. The old covenant was not erased. It was transformed. The brokenness of the past became a talisman for the promises of the future.

In the same way, you can write a new covenant with your spouse that acknowledges the past while accepting the redemptive possibility of the future. Maybe you have chosen to renew your vows after you've come through a period of hardship. Or you might have a renewal ceremony when an important life passage has occurred, such as your children moving out of the house or getting married. Maybe you recognize that you were emotionally and spiritually asleep at your wedding. Maybe you look back on your vows and realize that the meaning you ascribed to your words was a lie. Now, awakened from the sleep, grown up and with eyes wide open, you want to make a commitment as the mature, truthful individuals you are. I did this when I got baptized a second time as an older teenager. My father didn't understand why it was necessary. I had been baptized as a baby and had my baptismal certificate. I explained to him that I had no recollection of the event, and while it may have meant a lot to the adults who gathered as witnesses, it meant absolutely nothing to me. This time it would be my choice, and it would have true meaning. It was my way of showing up to symbolize my connection with the Sacred.

That is what renewing your wedding vows can be like. You can create a new relationship that you are fully choosing with your informed and enlightened consent.

Before you renew your vows, it is important to acknowledge your marriage for what it has been. Write the story of your marriage, choosing themes that enhance your union: joy (at the birth of a child); struggle (through health crises and job losses); and overcoming barriers (infidelity, addiction, depression). Who have you been in the marriage? Who are you committed to becoming? What do you imagine it is like living with you? Asking these questions and finding answers is the beginning of a mature relationship.

Draw the time line of your years together, choosing a word or phrase to symbolize each year: *newness and passion . . . miscarriage . . . Mother's death . . . Jack's birth . . . laid off . . . work and contentment . . . our own house . . . loving and living . . . struggle and separation . . .* and so on. If you have done the work of this book, your reflection on the years past will resonate as milestones on an ongoing journey. Ask yourselves what the journey has taught you and your partner in its joys and sorrows, its stops and starts, its steep hills and low valleys, its green and lush pastures. As mature adults embarking on a new portion of the journey, accept your past without blame or shame. It is the training ground for success, if we allow it to be.

Use the worksheet below to organize your thoughts for each year. For additional years, make copies of the blank worksheet in the appendix.

FAMILY TIMELINE WORKSHEET

YEAR					
SYMBOLIC TITLE					
FAMILY MILESTONES					
WORK MILESTONES					
KEY STRUGGLE					
KEY TRIUMPH					
LESSON					

The vows you make in your renewal ceremony should acknowledge the journey you've taken. Before you write your vows, spend some time reflecting on your original wedding vows:

When you promised to love, honor, and cherish each other, what did that mean to you then? What does it mean to you now?

When you promised to forsake all others, what did that mean to you then? How has your understanding changed? Do you feel differently now?

When you vowed to be committed for better or worse, what did that mean to you? How do you interpret this vow and its meaning today?

What significance did your vow to be united for richer or poorer hold for you? How has its meaning changed?

What commitment were you making when you vowed to be together in sickness and health? What have you learned from experience that gives new meaning to that vow?

When you made the solemn promise to be married until death, what did it mean to you? Has your life experience altered your view of what that promise means?

Review the elements of intentional vow creation in Chapter Ten. These are relevant to vow renewal as well, but within the context of your history. As you write your vows of renewal, you can speak a truth that was not available to you before.

Here are some examples of how you can transform your past lies into new truths through your vows:

Twenty-five years ago, I promised to love and cherish you, for better or worse, but I secretly expected it to always be better, and I let you down sometimes when things were hard. I promised to love you for richer or poorer, but I counted on riches—if not material, then emotional. When the well has been dry, I've sometimes let my disappointment show, punished you with my distance, and turned away from you.

I promised to love you in sickness and health, but I harbored a fantasy that the bloom of our youth would never fade, and I wasn't always willing to take care of you or of myself, or to resist judgment about the physical effects of aging. When you needed me to go the extra mile, I know I disappointed you and stopped halfway.

I promised to love you until death, but along the way, I took many exits and sometimes closed the door behind me, leaving you afraid and alone. Today I stand before you and renew those vows, secure in their truth. The joy I feel today is different from the joy I felt when I stood at the altar and gave you my heart twenty-five years ago. I know now what I didn't fully know then—that our love is true, through good times and bad. I renew my vows today, with my mind, body, and heart fully open to you.

Twenty-five years ago, when I stood at this altar and promised to love and cherish you until the day I died, I was filled with happiness to know that you would share my life. But there was so much I didn't know. I didn't know that love could survive when feelings failed, or how easy it would be to emotionally withdraw or fantasize about a different reality. I didn't expect my tolerance to be tested by life's trials. I didn't know that the suitcases we packed for our new life together would contain the baggage of our past, and that when we hurt, we would retreat into licking our old wounds. All those years ago, I made my vows to you, hoping for the best. Today I renew those vows in truth. I can say now that I know you, and I choose you all over again. For the rest of my life, I vow to find ways to cherish you, to express my love every day, to listen to you and understand you, to support your dreams and your freedom, to do what I can to make our home a place of trust and truth. I vow to love, honor, and respect our differences, the ways in which we are unique and separate, and to not insult the sacredness of your individuality or my own by trying to change you or myself. I will work on being a healthy and growing self who offers myself to another healthy and growing self.

Make your renewal wedding ceremony inclusive of others—family, friends, and especially other couples, who can reflect on their own intentions by bearing witness to your desire to renew your commitment. I have found that marriage renewal ceremonies can have an electrifying effect on the other couples present, especially if the ceremonies are intentional. They are a gift you can give to the people in your circle.

Involve your children and grandchildren in the renewal ceremony—not in the exchange of vows, which is exclusive to the marriage, but as witnesses. Older children and adult children can participate by making a statement, reciting a prayer or poem, or reading a letter they've written to both of you about the significance of being a family and what your union has meant to them, in both its joy and sorrow, its triumphs and defeats. Your renewal ceremony will become an event where the whole family and those gathered as witnesses enter the holy realm of living and speaking more in truth than in lies. It will be a priceless gift for all who are privileged to participate.

When you stand together in the presence of the community and renew your vows, a life of possibility opens up to you. You see with clear eyes: It's not another man. It's not another woman. It's you. The same people. But everything has been transformed.

RITUALS OF RENEWAL

What are some of the practices you can bring into your renewed marriage that will keep you mindful of your vows? Remember, the important thing about rituals is that they transcend feelings. They're intentionally repeated, through good times and bad, making them a habit, like your commitment to each other. Both good and bad habits are created by repetition and intention. You want to create habits that support your marriage of restoration and new life by repeating attitudes, behaviors, and actions that reinforce the mature, passionate marriage you are committed to creating. Practice these behaviors until they become second nature.

Restore rituals that brought you together. Couples often complain, "We used to talk on the phone every night, and now we barely speak." Or "We used to love to go out dancing, but it's been years since we danced." Consider the small gestures and everyday activities that solidified your togetherness when you started out as a couple. Ask yourself how you can restore some of these rituals, either in the same form as the past, or in a different form that suits both of you in the present. You must nurture yourself, each other, and your relationship. You can't starve your relationship of truth, respect, joy, and honor, and think that your marriage will grow into a passionate-alive union. Marriage, like all living things, requires sustenance.

What each of us longs for is to have another person who stands before us as a witness to our life. Of the billions of humans on the planet, the masses of humanity, living and dead, this one other really sees us, shines a light on our truth. And we in turn see him or her. Although we are insignificant in the vast scheme of things, we can, through an intimate bond, know what it means to really matter. This is the promise of every marriage. You can make it the promise of yours.

Twelve

"A CANDLE LOSES NOTHING BY
LIGHTING ANOTHER CANDLE."
—Chinese Proverb

Light Three Candles

The journey we have taken in this book has been a process of awakening. You have been invited to live in truth, to know yourself and your partner, and to probe beyond your comfort zone. You have been encouraged to stretch yourself into emotional and relational maturity. Stretching is a process, but like anything else, the more you do it, the more limber your emotional muscles become. As you begin this process of showing up, growing yourself up, and pushing past old wounds, the stretching may feel like it's going to break you, but it won't. What it will do is break the old habits and patterns that have prevented you from achieving a satisfying, loving, and rewarding intimate relationship. Don't let your discomfort deceive you into thinking that you're stretching too much. What you're really doing is stretching yourself into the person you were born to be. You are stretching yourself into the intimate partner who is a witness to the life of the one whom you love. And, for the sake of your children, you are stretching yourself into a healthy, mature parent who provides nurture and possibility, not injury. This is my charge to you—and it is a charge I have accepted for myself. We must do this to save ourselves, our children, our marriages, and our planet!

But we cannot be expected to accomplish all of this in the dark, or in the dim flicker of fear and weakness. So I will leave you with one final secret: When you light three candles, the path to a great marriage and a great life will be illuminated.

YOUR THREE CANDLES

Many of us come to relationships feeling that we do not have enough light within ourselves to live. We are looking for another person to show us the way. In my own family, we all learned to bask in the reflected glow of my father's light. He was a magnificent man—smart, successful, well respected, kind, and oh so gentle. My mother was content to live in his light, and so was I, even though we couldn't always see well when he wasn't around. My mother taught me that I needed a man to hold a light over me. She didn't realize that I could hold my own light—that I could live my life through *me*, not through a man. It took me a long time to find my light.

I often hear women talking about how they feel incomplete without a man, or men describing their wives as "my better half," as if they had been only a partial, lesser person before marriage. They are so relieved when they meet another person who wants to be with them that they extinguish their own candle and say, in effect, "I am yours."

The romantic fantasy that in marriage "two become one" is a dangerous construct if it means that one of you will disappear, your unique flame snuffed out. When only one candle burns, a self has been sacrificed to another's needs and desires.

The only way to begin a successful relationship is when both people come to it as complete human beings who carry their own strong candles of light. But even this is not enough. How many couples tell each other, "You go your way, and I'll go mine, and maybe we'll meet in the middle." The idea of being separate yet joined can be confusing, since there are so few models to show us the way. I know many couples for whom the home front is essentially the woman's domain, and even when she works outside the home, she runs the household and coordinates the children's lives. The man doesn't know the names of his children's best friends or where the extra toothpaste is kept, because his domain is the office. They are ships passing in the night, and though their lives may run smoothly, they are essentially separate. With time, they each begin asking, "Is it good for *me*?" Not "Is it good for the relationship?"

In my practice, I hear people say, "I feel alone in this marriage," because the vital connection has been broken. They've stopped talking, stopped making love, stopped sharing their dreams for the future. They've drifted so far apart on the path that they can no longer see the flicker of each other's candles.

No marriage can thrive when only two candles are lit—one for "you" and one for "me." Two candles represent the glow of individuals revolving in their own spheres.

In Marc Chagall's mesmerizing painting *Three Candles*, a young couple stands in the glow of three tall candles. Their arms are linked tightly, and they seem to be lifted off the earth yet at the same time grounded. The terrain around them appears both magical and utterly real. This is the mystery and wonder of a marriage that exists in the light of three candles. Two separate and fully alive individuals can agree to travel the same path together. Not to supply what's missing but to enhance what's already there. To say not "You make me better," but "In your presence, I want to be my best."

A marriage that lights three candles is a wonderful invitation to grow and live your best life. The words of Jean-Paul Sartre have become a guiding force for me: "At the moment of commitment, the Universe will conspire to assist you." I invite you to embrace these bold words and make your first vow to the relationship that you will discover, create, and nurture with the universe. It is with the assistance and cooperation of this steady relationship anchor that you can be a whole individual who can fully and freely offer another individual a place of shelter, rest, growth, and joy in a union that is primed to thrive.

You can change your life, your circumstances, your attitude, your condition, and the flow of energy in your intimate relationship. You can overcome the roadblocks in your life, and work through things that you thought had permanently stolen your joy. You can purge the cheating lies that have crushed your opportunities to create a lasting and fulfilling love connection. But we all need assistance, we need a positive conspiracy and backing, we need the help of the Universe in these sacred endeavors.

I believe that Sartre's words were saying that all the forces of the Universe will be at your disposal, but the offer is conditional on your commitment to do the hard work of examining your life and your relationship, and getting real and true with yourself and your partner. Seek to understand the original source of pain that keeps showing up as a blockage in your relationships, knowing that you can't fix what you don't acknowledge. Then take different actions than those that have kept you in a rut and prevented a rich, fulfilling relationship.

Humility, identification, acknowledgment, and treatment of the problematic and painful issues will lead to a prognosis of a healthy, whole, and fulfilled individual who is capable and equipped to create a strong and happy intimate love connection. There is no easy answer to complex pain, and life will not allow you to soothe sacred wounds with cheap surrogates. You have to do the work of healing. The reward is great, and everything is at stake—your ability and birthright to live your best life!

So, partner with the wise power of the Universe. When you show up as a grown-up, it will conspire in awesome ways to assist you! I'll be looking for you on this promising journey toward aliveness. It will be the best investment of your life.

Appendix

Marriage Exercises

In this appendix, you will find selected backup exercise forms, with suggestions about how to use them throughout your life as part of the ongoing process of growing in your marriage. For more insight, I encourage you to go back and read the relevant chapters as you use them. If you are not married, I'll recommend ways you can apply the exercises to grow yourself so you can be fully present in all of your relationships. The first step to attracting a healthy partner is to become a healthy person, not as a strategy for closing a deal on finding a great mate, but because you realize that you deserve to be happy and healthy for yourself.

SHOW UP AND GROW UP

Exercise 1: **YOUR INNER DOWRY**

The most valuable dowry you can bring to a marriage is yourself, fully awake and engaged. This exercise involves the emotional, spiritual, intellectual, sensual, and physical riches each of you brings to the marriage. Even if you have been

Exercise continued on next page

married for a long time, it is not too late to recommit with the presentation of a new dowry.

Five positive qualities you are bringing to the marriage:

1.

2.

3.

4.

5.

Five positive qualities your partner is bringing to the marriage:

1.

2.

3.

4.

5.

Review each other's lists, and have a conversation about what the "items" mean to you. Are there missing items you need to ask for? Are there items on your partner's list that don't represent you?

Exercise 2: REPACK YOUR HOPE CHEST

As we have learned, hope without action is like a feather on the wind. It is meaningless. So your hope chest must also be packed with actions—the intentional practices that will give substance to your hopes. Repack your hope chest every year, every five years, or whenever you feel the need to refresh your intentions.

If you are not married but hope to be someday, pack your chest with the practices that will make you stronger and fully realized in your own life. If you are married, pack the chest together as the actualization and reaffirmation of your commitment to a passionate and mature love connection.

My/our hope chest is filled with . . .

TO LOVE, HONOR, AND CHERISH

Exercise 1: DEFINING LOVE IN ACTION

Practicing the vow to love, honor, and cherish involves being aware of how you express and experience those actions. Stop every so often throughout your married life to remind yourselves of what these concepts mean to you.

Even if you are not married or currently in a relationship, this exercise reinforces the fact that you are worthy of love and respect in your life, and that you can give it to others. It will strengthen you and make you less likely to invest in any relationship where you are not valued, or which re-creates the hurt of unmet childhood needs.

I experience LOVE when you _____.
I experience HONOR when you _____.
I experience being CHERISHED when you _____.

I express LOVE when I _____.
I express HONOR when I _____.
I express that I CHERISH my partner when I _____.

I experience LOVE when you _____.
I experience HONOR when you _____.
I experience being CHERISHED when you _____.

I express LOVE when I _____.
I express HONOR when I _____.
I express that I CHERISH my partner when I _____.

FORSAKING ALL OTHERS

Exercise 1: SET YOUR MARRIAGE TABLE

In the course of your lives, you will reset your Marriage Table many times. I suggest that you establish a date once a year (not

Exercise continued on next page

your anniversary, New Year's Day, or other significant dates) when you will review the place cards and make changes. You can also reset your Marriage Table as people come and go in your lives—as children are born, jobs change, moves occur, and loved ones transition and pass away.

The Marriage Table exercise can be modified for those who are unmarried. Every person must make choices about which people to hold close, which to have limited relationships with, and which to turn away from. Doing this exercise can help you resolve issues in your family, close doors on unhealthy relationships, and call forth the voices that enhance and inspire you.

STEP 1: Sit down together and list all the people who are seated at your Marriage Table. These are the people (living and dead) who play a role in your lives, such as:

Parents
Siblings
Extended family
Ex-spouses/girlfriends/boyfriends
Children from previous marriages
Friends, both male and female
Clergy
Bosses
Colleagues
Neighbors
Beloved pets
Past influences
Hurtful relationships

STEP 2: When you have created your joint list, take some time individually to place the names around your table. On separate sheets of paper, draw a big rectangular shape, representing your table. Place you and your partner at the center. Then, spreading out from each side, write the names from your list, as if you were making place cards for your table.

Exercise continued on next page

STEP 3: Share your results. How do your seating plans at the Marriage Table differ? Talk about your reasons for seating people where you did. Are there people who don't belong at your Marriage Table at all? Be honest about describing the roles others will play in your lives. Are there surprise guests, or guests one of you doesn't think should be welcomed?

STEP 4: Take a third sheet of paper and draw a new rectangular shape. This will be the table you set together. Take plenty of time making your final seating arrangements at the Marriage Table. You may want to work on it over the course of a week or two, until you're both satisfied. Keep in mind that your Marriage Table seating plan isn't permanent. You can—and should—reset it as your lives change.

FOR BETTER OR WORSE

Exercise 1: **YOUR TOTAL REPAIR KIT**

When a pipe breaks or a screw loosens or a chair leg wobbles, you get out your tools and fix it. If you don't have a tool kit, or crucial tools are missing, you cannot make the repair.

Sit down with your partner and make a list of what you need on hand for the hard times. Your kit should include qualities such as compassion, humor, and the willingness to listen; necessities such as a good night's sleep and a healthy meal; and practices such as a mirroring exercise.

Every person should have a repair kit on hand. Pipes break for unmarried people, too! Be sure to have your repair kit well stocked, so you aren't overly reliant on others or desperate for rescue.

Our/my repair kit includes . . .

FOR RICHER OR POORER

Exercise 1: PRIORITIES CHECKLIST

Your financial status and priorities will change throughout your life. Perform this exercise once a year, before you settle on a budget.

The chart below lists typical expenses. To the right of each item are numbers reflecting a scale of importance from 1 (less important) to 3 (more important) to 5 (most important). Individually mark the number that matches your personal priorities, then compare.

Name_____ Priorities Checklist				
Owning a house	1	2	3	4	5
Automobiles	1	2	3	4	5
Savings	1	2	3	4	5
Training/education	1	2	3	4	5
Having children	1	2	3	4	5
Health care	1	2	3	4	5
Clothing	1	2	3	4	5
Home improvement	1	2	3	4	5
Furniture	1	2	3	4	5
Supporting relatives	1	2	3	4	5
Travel	1	2	3	4	5
Entertainment	1	2	3	4	5
Cosmetic goods/procedures	1	2	3	4	5

Exercise continued on next page

Prior debts	1	2	3	4	5
Pets	1	2	3	4	5
Hobbies	1	2	3	4	5
Electronic equipment	1	2	3	4	5
Holidays/celebrations	1	2	3	4	5
Charity	1	2	3	4	5
Fitness	1	2	3	4	5
Other_____	1	2	3	4	5

Exercise 2: **YOUR MARITAL ATM**

Couples slip into routines, and it's typical for one person to invest more and the other to invest less, at different times. If you try to withdraw cash from the ATM and you haven't deposited money into your account, you'll receive a message: "Insufficient funds." The same is true in marriage. If one person is making most of the deposits (of time, money, and love), while the other is always withdrawing those funds, you need to balance your account.

You don't have to be married to benefit from performing this exercise. In all important relationships, there are givers and takers. It helps to clarify for yourself whether you are overinvesting or overwithdrawing from the ATM of your life.

Partner 1

Think about the past week. List five credits you put into your marital ATM. (For example, you cooked dinner three times and took your mother-in-law shopping without complaining.)

1.

Exercise continued on next page

2.

3.

4.

5.

List five debits you took out of your marital ATM. (For example, you talked about your work problems for an hour, or you slept in while your partner fixed breakfast.)

1.

2.

3.

4.

5.

Partner 2

Think about the past week. List five credits you put into your marital ATM. (For example, you cooked dinner three times and took your mother-in-law shopping without complaining.)

1.

2.

3.

4.

5.

List five debits you took out of your marital ATM. (For example, you talked about your work problems for an hour, or you slept in while your partner fixed breakfast.)

1.

2.

3.

4.

5.

Compare your lists. If there is balance, good for you. If there is imbalance, decide what investment the "overdrawn" partner will make.

MARRIAGE VOWS

INTENTIONAL VOW WRITING

As you write your vows, this formula can help you put your true intentions into words.

I promise to [state your truth] _____,
to [accept your and my individuality and needs] _____,
to [acknowledge our brokenness and possibility] _____,
to [embrace the world around us] _____.

CREATE LIVING VOWS

True vows are expressed through regular day-to-day practices.
Examine your vows and designate practices that will keep them alive.

Promise	Practice

MARRIAGE VOW RENEWAL

MARRIAGE TIME LINE

Tell the story of your marriage, using the form below to organize your thoughts for each year. Make copies for additional years and keep them in a family notebook.

Exercise continued on next page

FAMILY TIME LINE WORKSHEET

Year				
Symbolic Title				
Family Milestones				
Work Milestones				
Key Struggle				
Key Triumph				
Lesson				

VOW RENEWAL FORM

When you renew your vows from a place of truth and maturity, you may find that your original vows lacked meaning and intention, or that they did not reflect promises you wanted to make or were able to keep. As you prepare to renew your vows, think back to your wedding vows and write down how you would frame your truth today.

Marriage Vow	New Vow

INDEX

F

failure, transformation of,
155–56
false repairs, 104–5
family:
children from previous
marriages, 76–79
at Marriage Table, 69–70, 71,
81–83, 215–17
money attitudes from,
110–11, 120–21
parents, 71–76, 80–81
questions to ask your partner
about, 168
rules on relationships with,
83–85
vow renewal and, 207
work attitudes from,
116–19
fantasy(ies), 28, 30–35, 60,
150–52, 187, 202, 210
abusers and, 154
con men and, 151–52
romantic, 30–35, 210
of shared qualities in others,
77
see also lies
fear, 52, 62, 92
of abandonment, 40, 71
of change, 41
of rejection, 15, 18
fidelity, 68
definition of, 85–86
sexual, 68–69, 85–86
firefighters, divorce among, 89
For Better or for Worse, 28–29
"forsaking all others," 68–87,
201
freedom, 24

friends, 79–80
at Marriage Table, 69–70, 71,
81–83, 168–69, 215–17
questions to ask your partner
about, 168–69
rules on relationships with,
83–85
vow renewal and, 207

G

Gandhi, Mahatma, 147
gender roles, questions to ask
your partner about, 180–81
giving and receiving line, 196–97
goodness, 56, 57
Gottman, John, 17
Groundhog Day, 50, 51
grown-ups, 25–26, 38–45
childish love compared with
mature love, 40–41
quiz for, 43–44
growth, relationships as
incubators for, 155–56
Guinean proverb, 109

H

habits, 191–92, 207
healing, 212
relationships as incubators for,
155–56
health, 129–46
addictions, 1, 3, 140–44
attitudes about, 145–46
and meaning of care, 131–36
questions to ask your partner
about, 164–65
self-care and, 136–37
sexual, 137–40